# Yarn World
A crafter's guide to yarn shops everywhere

2016-2017

# Lisa Maness Prakash

First Edition

Peacock Press Books

Copyright 2015 by Lisa Maness Prakash
Saginaw, Michigan 48609
www.peacockpressbooks.com
peacockpressbooks@gmail.com

The author gratefully acknowledges the use of particular images and fonts, and has listed such in acknowledgements.

The Library of Congress has catalogued the soft cover edition as follows:
Library of Congress.in publication data
Prakash, Lisa Maness.
Yarn Travel/Lisa Maness Prakash
p. cm.
Includes index.
ISBN 978.0.692.41630.3
1. Yarn l. Prakash, Lisa ll.Title
Library of Congress Control Number: 2015943624

Book cover design and layout by Ellie Bockert Augsburger of Creative Digital Studios.
www.CreativeDigitalStudios.com

Cover design features:
Wool Balls: © potapenkoivan / Dollar Photo Club

First published in the United States by Peacock Press Books
First Printing

# Table of Contents

Introduction ............................................................................... 1
Types of Yarn Fibers .................................................................. 2
Wool 101 .................................................................................... 2
Grades of Wool .......................................................................... 5
Yarns 101 ................................................................................... 5

# North America

United States of America ......................................................... 8
Alabama ..................................................................................... 9
Alaska ........................................................................................ 9
Arizona ..................................................................................... 11
Arkansas .................................................................................. 12
California .................................................................................. 13
Colorado ................................................................................... 22
Connecticut .............................................................................. 26
Delaware ................................................................................... 28
District of Columbia ................................................................. 29
Florida ...................................................................................... 29
Georgia ..................................................................................... 32
Hawaii ....................................................................................... 35
Idaho ......................................................................................... 35
Illinois ....................................................................................... 37
Indiana ...................................................................................... 41
Iowa .......................................................................................... 43
Kansas ...................................................................................... 45
Kentucky .................................................................................. 46
Louisiana .................................................................................. 48

| | |
|---|---|
| Maine | 49 |
| Maryland | 52 |
| Massachusetts | 53 |
| Michigan | 57 |
| Minnesota | 63 |
| Mississippi | 67 |
| Missouri | 68 |
| Montana | 69 |
| Nebraska | 71 |
| Nevada | 72 |
| New Hampshire | 72 |
| New Jersey | 74 |
| New Mexico | 76 |
| New York | 78 |
| North Carolina | 86 |
| North Dakota | 90 |
| Ohio | 91 |
| Oklahoma | 96 |
| Oregon | 97 |
| Pennsylvania | 101 |
| Rhode Island | 106 |
| South Carolina | 107 |
| South Dakota | 108 |
| Tennessee | 109 |
| Texas | 110 |
| Utah | 114 |
| Vermont | 115 |
| Virginia | 117 |
| Washington | 120 |

West Virginia .................................................... 125
Wisconsin ......................................................... 125
Wyoming .......................................................... 129

Canada ............................................................. 132
Alberta .............................................................. 132
British Columbia ............................................... 132
Manitoba ........................................................... 132
New Brunswick ................................................. 133
Newfoundland ................................................... 133
Nova Scotia ....................................................... 133
Ontario .............................................................. 134
Niagara Falls Area ............................................ 135
Prince Edward Island ....................................... 136
Quebec .............................................................. 136
Saskatchewan ................................................... 137
Yukon ................................................................ 137

Mexico ............................................................... 138
Nuevo Leon ....................................................... 138
Jalisco ................................................................ 138
Tecate ................................................................ 138

The Caribbean .................................................. 139
Aruba ................................................................. 139
Barbados ........................................................... 139
Bermuda ............................................................ 139
Cayman Islands ................................................. 139
Puerto Rico ....................................................... 139

Trinidad & Tobago .................................................................................. 140
Central America ...................................................................................... 141
Costa Rica ................................................................................................ 141

# Good Stuff to Know

Crochet Master List .................................................................................142
Knitting Master List ................................................................................144
Other Yarn 101 ........................................................................................147
Standard Yarn Weight System ...............................................................149
U.S. Fiber Shows/Conventions .............................................................150
International Fiber Shows/Knitting Excursions.................................154
Cruises ...................................................................................................... 161

# Europe

Austria ......................................................................................................164
Belgium ....................................................................................................164
Cyprus ......................................................................................................165
Czech Republic .......................................................................................165
Denmark...................................................................................................165
England ....................................................................................................166
Finland ..................................................................................................... 167
France....................................................................................................... 168
Germany ..................................................................................................169
Greece ....................................................................................................... 171
Hungary.................................................................................................... 171
Ireland ...................................................................................................... 172
Northern Ireland .................................................................................... 173
Italy ........................................................................................................... 173

Netherlands ........................................................................................... 174
Norway ................................................................................................. 175
Poland .................................................................................................. 176
Portugal ............................................................................................... 176
Russia .................................................................................................. 176
Scotland .............................................................................................. 177
Spain .................................................................................................... 178
Sweden ................................................................................................ 179
Switzerland ........................................................................................ 179
Turkey .................................................................................................. 180
Wales ................................................................................................... 180

# South America

Argentina ............................................................................................ 185
Brazil .................................................................................................... 185
Chile ..................................................................................................... 185
Colombia ............................................................................................ 186
Peru ..................................................................................................... 187
Uruguay .............................................................................................. 187

# Africa

Egypt ................................................................................................... 188
Kenya .................................................................................................. 188
South Africa ...................................................................................... 188

# Asia

Bahrain ............................................................................................... 190
Brunei .................................................................................................. 191
Cambodia .......................................................................................... 191

| | |
|---|---|
| China | 192 |
| Estonia | 194 |
| Indonesia | 197 |
| Israel | 198 |
| Japan | 199 |
| Kuwait | 200 |
| Lebanon | 201 |
| Malaysia | 201 |
| Nepal | 201 |
| Pakistan | 201 |
| Philippines | 202 |
| Qatar | 202 |
| Saudi Arabia | 202 |
| Singapore | 203 |
| South Korea | 203 |
| Taiwan | 203 |
| Thailand | 204 |
| United Arab Emirates | 205 |
| Vietnam | 205 |

# Australia/New Zealand

| | |
|---|---|
| Australia | 206 |
| New Zealand | 208 |

# More Information

| | |
|---|---|
| Acknowledgements | 209 |
| More Information/Contact | 210 |
| Notes | 211 |

# Introduction

There is no greater feeling for a yarn junkie than walking into a shop full of hand painted beautiful yarns and fibers of all colors. Breathe deeply and take it all in, then let it all out. Touch them. It is the promise of yet another fabulous project or just simply a need to buy more stash for those projects we might create "down the road". I know very few people who have the willpower to walk into a yarn shop and walk out with their hands empty. You know what I am talking about- we are all guilty.

And traveling can be fun too and for yarn hoarders like myself, it is better than fun. It is a blast! More stash!!

What better way to compliment your travels than by collecting yarns from around the world while traveling the world? As a knitter who started late in life (42), I wasted no time in learning the meaning of stash. I covet fine yarns from Japan to New Mexico to Peru and back. This is why I could wait no longer to publish a guide for you to find the best of yarns no matter where you are or where you travel. Yarn knows no boundaries. From uptown New York, to alpaca farms in Vermont to Bangladesh's women's cooperatives, yarn is everywhere--even Beverly Hills has a yarn boutique!

Every single listing in this book has been verified by me personally as of June 2015. Sadly, what I have learned in this business, is that yarn shops come and go. Please note that as I try to be as accurate as possible, there will be yarn shops that are no longer in business since this book has gone to print. Therefore, it is recommended that you call <u>prior</u> to visiting the shop to avoid disappointment.

Have fun and always carve out enough time in your travels to enjoy a yarn shop!

# Types of Yarn Fibers

(Trying to Make Sense of it All)

All types of yarns used for knitting or crocheting are made from natural or synthetic fibers. Different types of yarn fibers have specific qualities — some good, some not so good. Review my list below so that when shopping for wool, you will have a better idea of what you are looking for before you spend your money.

## Wool 101

**Wool** is the textile fiber obtained from sheep and certain other animals, including cashmere from goats, mohair from goats, qiviut from muskoxen, and angora from rabbits. Wool is the most popular yarn among knitters and crocheters, and is used for hats, socks, sweaters and other clothing and accessories.

**Alpaca** is, as it says, from the alpaca. This fine silky fabric is warmer than sheep wool. Knit or crochet sweaters, gloves, and scarves with this wonderful fiber. Personally, I love using baby alpaca yarn-it is extra soft!

**Angora** is made from the hair of the Angora rabbit. This heat-retaining fiber is ideal for thermal clothing. As lightweight as it is soft, it's very comfortable to wear, making an ideal yarn for sweaters, blankets and hats. (Another softy yarn!)

**Camel Hair** (I was surprised about this one and can't say I have seen this in any local yarn shop.) As you would expect, camel hair comes from a camel. The undercoat of the Bactrian camel is extremely soft and fine, making it a good choice for clothing. Camel hair provides the best insulation of all the wools, so it is usually used for coats. These specific camels are often found in Turkey and other parts of Asia. This is considered an exotic yarn and can be purchased online. Coats and carpets are often made of this hair.

**Cashgora** is a hybrid wool, which comes from a crossbreed of a Cashmere buck and an Angora doe. You'll find it finer than mohair but less so than cashmere.

**Cashmere** comes from the hair of a Kashmir (or cashmere) goat. Soft to the touch, so it is a pleasure to wear. It is also extremely adept at keeping you warm. Who would turn down a cashmere sweater??

**Lamb's wool** tends to be warmer and a bit itchy, yet holds its shape. The biggest distinction of lamb's wool is that it is considered virgin and is shorn from a seven month old baby lamb. This is considered the lamb's first shearing and has excellent spinning qualities. It is a favorite for blankets and sweaters.

**Llama** is part of the camel family, thus this exotic yarn creates a naturally warm, high-quality yarn. Llama yarn has a high thermal capacity, lightness and high wear durability making it a very desirable yarn for hats and coats. It is warm without being too heavy.

**Merino wool** has a beautiful shine to it and is incredibly soft. Merino sheep are known to have softer coats and draws moisture away from the skin on one end of the fiber and repels outside moisture on the other. Merino wool is very white in its original form and dyes well. You won't get any itchiness from this wool due to its fineness, which makes me a happy girl!

**Mohair** is wool that comes from the Angora goat, which is not to be confused with Angora that comes from the Angora rabbit. It is coarser than cashmere but it wears well and responds beautifully to dyeing. Mohair fibers are moisture-wicking and good insulators, and wears better than sheep's wool.

**Pure new wool/virgin wool** is made directly from animal fleece and not recycled from existing wool garments. This wool has not been processed in any way. (See lamb's wool)

**Qiviut** is a grayish/brown colored fiber that comes from the Alaskan domesticated musk ox and is as soft as cashmere. While it weighs the same as sheep's wool, it's eight times warmer. Got allergies? This fiber is hypoallergenic and considered rare. You'll see it used in sweaters, scarves, gloves, and hats if and when you ever find it.

**Shetland wool** is made from the small and hardy native sheep of Scotland's Shetland Islands on Scotland's northern coast. The wool these sheep produce is a very fine and lustrous wool, cultivated from their soft undercoat. This wool is usually found in natural colors, and is often used for coats, knitwear and sportswear.

**Washable wool** when washed, should not felt or shrink. Treated chemically, the process ensures that the scales will not bind.

# Grades of Wool

The type or grade of wool you select should meet the needs of the project you want to work on, so check out my list below to ensure that you have chosen the right grade for you. This will help you to get the terrific results you are looking for!

**Virgin Wool**: Taken from a lamb's first shearing, also virgin wool can refer to wool that has never been used, processed, or woven.

**Boiled Wool**: Created through a washing process applied to a knitted wool to make a dense, durable, and water resistant fabric. When I think of boiled wool, I think of pea coats and cold weather!

**Worsted Wool**: Manufactured in Worsted, England since the eighteenth century, wool fibers are spun into compact, smoothly twisted yarn before weaving or knitting.

# Yarns 101

**Bamboo** is a woody grass that is harvested and distilled into cellulose that is then spun into the yarn. Yarns that are pure bamboo are soft, silky to the touch, and have a subtle shine. The great thing about bamboo is that it is a sustainable resource that is easily renewed. It is another one of the warm weather yarns, so take your projects on your next trip to the beach! Personally, I just love bamboo –it is soft and easy to work when either knitting or crocheting. Blends of bamboo and silk are especially luxurious.

**Bouclé** is knitted with many purl stitches, producing tight fleece which is similar to a poodle coat, hence boucle yarn is also known as poodle yarn. It is available in different sizes. Oh how I love poodle coats!

**Brushed Fleece** is a super soft blend of extra fine merino wool and baby alpaca. The yarn has a soft marl color effect and is quick to knit making it very wearable, warm and lightweight.

**Cotton Yarn** is a personal favorite of mine, having grown up in a warm climate. Great for socks in the summer as well as wraps for a cool summer's night, cotton will never disappoint. A word of caution however, it can get heavy if you are making a blanket or sweater. It also has little elasticity and often, won't go back to its original shape. It is breathable, pulls water away from your body and is so easy to work with. My favorite for dishcloths too.

**Linen yarn** is a great choice for knitters who want durability and breathability. A favorite for warm climates, linen is classic and never goes out of style.

**Rayon** is a type of yarn that includes some rayon fiber, a type of man-made fiber produced from natural plant cellulose. It is cool, soft, and lightweight like bamboo or linen fiber. It is not insulating at all, which makes it a warm weather yarn. All rayon yarn is also relatively weak and prone to breakage, especially when it gets wet.

**Ribbon** can be made out of various materials, such as cotton, rayon or nylon. It is popular at the moment and often used to make vests, hats and sweaters.

**Silk** has been long regarded as the fabric of royalty. Yarn is a great way to add a touch of luxury to your otherwise standard, knitting patterns. It is also gorgeously soft and can be fashioned into apparel that will be appropriate and comfortable all year long. There are many different grades and types of silk qualities, such as reeled or filament. There are recycled sari yarn silks from India, which by the way, make beautiful bags.

*Novelty Yarns* are a fun addition to any project and are easy to recognize because their appearance is so different from traditional yarns. Here are a few samples:

**Chenille** brings back lovely memories. I recall as a child visiting my grandmother and sleeping on her chenille bedspread. Ahhh... so velvety! It is worth it to work with, although a bit tricky.

**Eyelash Yarn:** This looks just like it sounds. Usually used as a trim on a project, it can be knitted up on its own, though you will most likely have to use two strands at a time. Often knitted using another yarn, such as chunky.

**Faux fur** is what it says it is, faux or fake. A great alternative to real fur, this faux fur is a fun way to add pizzazz to trim scarves, gloves, or hats. It is just plain fun!

**Railroad Ribbon** has tiny "tracks" of fiber strung between two parallel strands of thread. Because it is a little different from your traditional yarn, I recommend using YouTube to get instructions for casting on and off.

# North America
# United States of America

# Alabama

**Andalusia**
Pale Moon Yarns
209 S. Three Notch Street
☎ 334.222.7253

**Birmingham**
Kollage Yarns
3591 Cahaba Beach Road
☎ 205.408.5815

In The Making
4232 Dolly Ridge Road #100
☎ 205.298.1309

**Boaz**
Wilson's Fabrics
1524 US Highway 431 N.
☎ 256.593.6501

**Enterprise**
Wiregrass Yarn Shop
704 Glover Avenue
☎ 334.308.9276

**Florence**
Unraveled Yarn and Gifts
215 N. Court Street
☎ 256.349.2533

**Foley**
Clara's Loom
7518 Riverwood Drive
☎ 251.943.2960

**Gadsden**
The Taming of the Ewe
106 6th Street
☎ 256.546.9090

**Harvest**
Little Barn
173 McKee Road
☎ 256.852.3366

**Huntsville**
Fiber Art Work
3004 Governors Drive SW
☎ 256.656.0163

**Jacksonville**
Yarns by Home Place Farm
402 Pelham Road N.
☎ 256.452.520

# Alaska

**Anchorage**
Far North Fibers
3960 Doroshin Avenue
☎ 907.279.0332

Far North Yarn Co.
2636 Spenard Road
Suite 6
☎ 907.258.5648

**Cordova**
The Net Loft
140 Adams Street
☎ 907.424.7337

**Eagle River**
The Tangled Skein
11753 Celestial Street
☎ 907.622.9276

**Fairbanks**
A Weaver's Yarn
1810 Alaska Way
☎ 907.374.1995

Inua Wool Shoppe
3677 College Road #3
☎ 907.479.5830

Northern Threads
1875 University Avenue
Suite 2
☎ 907.455.0299

**Haines**
Dalton City Yarn Emporium
296 Fair Drive
☎ 907.766.2779

Material Girls
322 Main Street
☎ 907.766.3391

**Healy**
Granma's Quilt Shop
4 Coal Street
☎ 907.683.2200

**Homer**
Commuknitty Stash
3581 B. Main Street
☎ 907.299.0601

**Juneau**
Forget Me Knots
9105 Mendenhall Mall
☎ 907.500.9950

Seaside Yarns
175 South Franklin Street
☎ 907.723.9227

**Ketchikan**
The Point
25 Jefferson Way
Suite 102B
☎ 907.225.2858

**Kodiak**
The Rookery
104 Center Avenue
Suite 100
☎ 907.486.0052

**North Pole**
Ben Franklin
301 N. Santa Claus Lane
Suite 16
☎ 907.488.8544

**Palmer**
Fantastic Fibers
1035 South Cobb Street
☎ 907.745.7295

**Seward**
A Flyin' Skein
223 Fourth Avenue
☎ 907.224.5648

**Sitka**
Knitting with Class
300 Harbor Drive
☎ 907.738.0957

**Skagway**
Aurora Yarns of Alaska
7th and Broadway
☎ 907.612.0083

Changing Threads
Seventh Avenue/Broadway
(May-September)
☎ 907.983.2397

Soldotna Birch Tree Gallery
48568 Funny River Road
☎ 907.262.4048

# Arizona

**Carefree**
Bonnie's Yarn Crafts
37555 Hum Road
☎ 480.595.7229

**Casa Grande**
Betty's Stitchery
517 E. Florence Boulevard
☎ 520.423.0202

**Flagstaff**
Purl In The Pines
2544 N. 4th Street
☎ 928.774.9334

**Fountain Hills**
Just Bead it AZ
16733 S. Lindsay Road
☎ 480.816.5914

**Gilbert**
Arizona Yarn and Fiber
3133 S. Lindsay Road #107
☎ 480.917.9276

**Glendale**
Sally Knits
6823 N. 58th Avenue
☎ 623.934.8367

**Jerome**
Knit1 Bead2
301 Main Street
☎ 928.634.7236

**Kingman**
The Spinster
116 N. 4th Street
☎ 928.753.3660

**Lake Havasu City**
The Yarn Shoppe
2069 McCulloch Boulevard
Suite 2
☎ 928.680.8689

**Mesa**
The Fiber Factory
216 W. Main Street
☎ 480.969.4346

**Phoenix**
Family Arts Needlework Shop
5555 N. 7th Street
Suite 144
☎ 602.277.0694

Phoenix Knits
5044 B Seventh Street
☎ 602.277.1335

**Prescott**
A Good Yarn/Fiber Creek
371 Garden Street
Suite D
☎ 928.717.1774

Studio Three
1440 W. Gurley Street
☎ 928.778.0307

**Safford**
Cotton Clouds
5176 S. 14th Avenue
☎ 928.428.7000

**Scottsdale**
Jessica Knits
8660 E. Shea Boulevard
Suite 170
☎ 480.515.4454

**Sedona**
The Sedona Knit Wits
3100 W. Highway 89A
☎ 928.282.3389

**Sierra Vista**
Squirrel's Nest
530 Bartow Drive
☎ 520.417.1070

**Tempe**
Tempe Yarn and Fiber
1415 E. University Drive
Suite A102
☎ 480.557.9166

**Tucson**
Grandma's Spinning Wheel
6544 E. Tanque Verde Road
#150
☎ 520.290.3738

Kiwi Knitting
2540 E. 6th Street
☎ 952.240.5646

Purls Tucson
7531 E. Broadway
☎ 520.296.6363

Tucson Yarn Company
6336 N. Oracle Road
Suite 302 C
☎ 520.229.9276

**Wiox**
World Wide Hobbies
100 S. Haskell Avenue
☎ 520.384.3197

# Arkansas

**Arkadelphia**
Knit Unto Others
323 Main Street
☎ 870.245.2552

**Batesville**
Marshall Dry Goods Company
310 W. Main Street
☎ 870.793.2405

**Bentonville**
The Sheep's Fleece Yarns
2800 SW 14th Street
Suite 6
☎ 479.273.1065

**Bull Shoals**
Gabriele's Flowers and Fibers
904 Central Boulevard
☎ 870.445.4273

**Eureka Springs**
Little Bo Peep's Yarn and
Antiques & Red Scottie Fibers
51 Spring Street
☎ 479.253.0711

**Fayettville**
Hand-Held A Knitting Gallery
15 N. Block Avenue
☎ 479.582.2910

**Harrison**
Deb's Frames and Things
102 W. Stephenson Avenue
☎ 870.741.6070

Sugar Gems
410 N. Main Street
☎ 870.688.4337

**Holiday Island**
Sew In Heaven
3 Parkcliff Drive
☎ 479.253.0770

**Hot Springs**
Knittin on the Corner
801 Central Avenue #11
☎ 501.623.2001

**Little Rock**
The Yarn Mart
5711 Kavanaugh Boulevard
☎ 501.666.6505

**Rogers**
Mockingbird Moon
315 North 2nd Street
☎ 479.202.5640

The Rabbit's Lair
116 S. First Street
☎ 479.636.3385

**Russellville**
Knit 2 Together
2300 W. Main Street
Suite 6
☎ 479.968.5648

**Siloam Springs**
Sager Creek Quilts & Yarn Works
304 East Central Street
☎ 479.524.5244

# California

**Alameda**
Alameda Yarn Company
2002 Encinal Avenue
☎ 510.523.9003

**Albany**
K2tog
1325 Solano Avenue
☎ 510.526.9276

**Anaheim**
Newton's Knits
2100 E. Howell Avenue #211
☎ 714.634.9116

**Apple Valley**
Fanciwerks Yarn Shoppe
21810 US Highway 18
Suite 2
☎ 760.961.0113

**Aptos**
Yarns by the Sea
7960 Soquel Drive #C
☎ 831.662.9276

**Arcata**
Fabric Temptations
942 G Street
☎ 707.822.7782

**Atascadero**
Ranch Dog Knitting
5835 Traffic Way
☎ 805.464.4075

**Auburn**
Auburn Needleworks
839 Lincoln Way
☎ 530.888.0202

**Avalon**
Catalina Crafters
115 Sumner Avenue
☎ 310.510.3590

**Azusa**
All about Yarn
607 E. Arrow Highway
☎ 626.967.2039

**Bakersfield**
Classy Knits and Yarns
1839 F Street
☎ 661.325.7226

Knit Happens Fine Yarns
200 Stine Road
☎ 661.396.8888

**Bellflower**
Stitches in Time
16525 Bellflower Boulevard
☎ 562.804.9341

**Benicia**
Fiber Frolics
637 1st Street
☎ 707.747.9276

**Berkeley**
Cakes and Purls
2115 Allston Way
☎ 510.225.0929

Claddagh Yarns
1506 Walnut Street
☎ 415.316.4276

**Beverly Hills**
Knitting House
260 South Beverly Drive #203
☎ 310.275.6438

**Big Bear City**
Yarn Designers Boutique
439 W. Big Bear Boulevard
☎ 909.584.9715

**Big Bear Lake**
Susan's Needlearts
42180 Moonridge Road
☎ 909.273.9874

**Bishop**
Sierra Cottons and Wools
117 E. Line Street
☎ 760.872.9209

**Bodega**
Artisans Co-Op
17135 A Bodega Highway
☎ 707.876.9830

**Burbank**
Unwind
818 N. Hollywood Way
☎ 818.840.0800

**Cambria**
Ball & Skein and More
4210 Bridge Street
☎ 805.927.3280

Flying Fuzzies
719 Main Street
☎ 805.927.2649

**Cedarville**
Warner Mountain Weavers
459 Main Street
☎ 530.279.2164

**Chico**
Heartstrings Yarn Studio
1909 Esplanade
☎ 530.894.1434

**Chula Vista**
Border Leather Corp.
261 Broadway
☎ 619.691.1657

**Claremont**
Colors 91711
248 Harvard Avenue
☎ 909.624.6161

Phebie's Needleart
532 W. First Street #210
☎ 909.624.5250

**Clovis**
The Knit Addiction
438 Pollasky Avenue
☎ 559.297.5648

**Corona**
Knit Affair Yarn Company
1690 W. Sixth Street
Unit O
☎ 951.738.0076

**Costa Mesa**
Suzoo's Wool Works
711 W. 17th Street F-9
☎ 949.574.0005

**Culver City**
The Knitting Tree, LA
6285 Bristol Parkway
☎ 310.395.3880

**Danville**
A Yarn Less Raveled
730 Camino Ramon
Suite 186
☎ 925.263.2661

Doodlebug
641 San Anselmo Avenue
☎ 415.456.5989

**Dublin**
That Yarn Store
7240 San Ramon Road
☎ 925.828.1327

**El Segundo**
The Split Stitch
421 Main Street
☎ 310.322.6793

## Elk Grove
Anna's Yarn Shoppe
at the Village
9635 E. Stockton Boulevard
☎ 916.747.4714

Knitique
8741 Elk Grove Boulevard
☎ 916.714.7719

## Emerald Hills
Amazing Yarns
2559 Woodland Place
☎ 650.306.9218

## Encinitas
The Black Sheep
1060 S. Coast Highway 101
☎ 760.436.9973

Common Threads
466 S. Coast Highway 101
☎ 760.436.6119

## Eureka
Northcoast Knittery
320 Second Street
Suite 1A
☎ 707.442.9276

Yarn
418 2nd Street
☎ 707.443.9276

## Fair Oaks
Babetta's Yarn Cafe
4400 San Juan Avenue
Suite 20
☎ 916.965.6043

## Fairfax
Doodlebug
641 San Anselmo Avenue
☎ 415.456.5989

Rainbow Fabrics Crafts and Things
50 Bolinas Road
☎ 415.459.5100

## Fortuno
Fortuno Fabrics Crafts and Things
2045 Main Street
☎ 707.725.2501

Generations
906 S. Fortuna
☎ 707.725.4293

## Fremont
Color Me Quilts and More
37495 Niles Boulevard
☎ 510.792.6567

## Fresno
Swatches
1764 W. Bullard Avenue
☎ 559.435.2813

## Ft. Bragg
Navarro River Knits
167 Boatyard Drive
☎ 707.964.9665

## Gardena
Let's Knit Yarn Shop
16126 S. Western Avenue
☎ 310.327.4514

**Glendale**
Itza Knitterie
1413 W. Kenneth Road
☎ 818.507.1813

**Glendora**
The PurlSide
1200 East Route 66, #109
☎ 626.914.3747

**Graeagle**
Wooly Notions
7580 Highway 89
House 118
☎ 530.836.1680

**Grass Valley**
A Star Alpacas
10521 Godfrey Lane
☎ 530.274.8748

**Half Moon Bay**
Elizabeth's Yarn Shop
80 Cabrillo Highway N.
Ste O
☎ 650.712.9276

Fengari
415 Main Street
☎ 650.726.2550

**Healdsburg**
Purls of joy
429 Healdsburg Avenue
☎ 707.433.5697

**Hemet**
Lazy Daisy Yarn Shop
2127 E. Florida Avenue
☎ 951.658.8134

**Jackson**
Sewing Cottage
11984 W. State Highway
☎ 209.223.0393

**Joshua Tree**
Knotty Knitters
7635 Vista Road
☎ 760.401.7084

**La Mesa**
Two Sisters and Ewe
8874 La Mesa Boulevard
☎ 619.460.8103

Yarn & Thread Expressions
7882 La Mesa Boulevard
☎ 619.460.9276

**Lafayette**
Busy Stix
3418 Mt. Diablo Boulevard
Suite A
☎ 925.284.1172

The Yarn Boutique
963C Moraga Road
☎ 925.283.7377

**Laguna Beach**
Strands and Stitches
1516 S. Coast Highway
☎ 949.497.5648

**Laguna Niguel**
TootsieP Yarns
31801 National Park Drive
☎ 949.300.8801

**Long Beach**
Alamitos Bay Yarn Company
174 N. Marina Drive
☎ 562.799.8484

**Los Altos**
Uncommon Threads
293 State Street
☎ 650.941.1815

**Los Angeles**
Gather DTLA
453 S. Spring Street
Ste M1
☎ 213.908.2656

Jennifer Knits
108 Barrington Walk
☎ 310.471.8733

Knit Culture Studio
8118 W. 3rd Street
☎ 323.655.6487

Little Knittery
3195 Glendale Boulevard
☎ 323.663.3838

Merceria Teresita
307 E. Jefferson Boulevard
☎ 323.233.8856

Michael Levine
920 S. Maple Avenue
☎ 213.622.6259

Needlepoints West
6227 W. 87th Street
☎ 310.670.4847

Zoe Zeynep Knit Studio
7201 Melrose Avenue
Suite B
☎ 323.936.7690

**Montrose**
Needle in a Haystack
2262 Honolulu Avenue
☎ 818.248.7686

**Morro Bay**
Morro Fleece Works
1920 Main Street
☎ 805.772.9665

**Mt. Shasta**
Weston's Quilting & Crafts
414 Chestnut Street
☎ 530.926.4021

**Pasadena**
Abuelita's Knitting &
Needlepoint
696 E. Colorado Boulevard
Suite 2
☎ 626.799.0355

**Placerville**
Lofty Lou's
585 Main Street
☎ 530.642.2270

**Pleasanton**
Knit This, Purl That!
205-A Main Street
☎ 925.249.9276

**Quincy**
The Woolroom
390 Jackson Street
☎ 530.283.0648

**Redlands**
Redlands Yarn Company
515 New Jersey Street
☎ 909.793.7301

Hands On Knitting Center
922 New York Street
☎ 909.793.8712

**Redwood City**
Amazing Yarn
2559 Woodland Place
☎ 650.306.9218

**Riverside**
Designer Hand Knits
Brockton Arcade
6730 Brockton Avenue
☎ 951.275.9711

Raincross Fiber Arts
3498 University Avenue
☎ 951.684.5647

**Roseville**
Got Your Goat
Rocky Ridge Town Center
2030 Douglas Boulevard #36
☎ 916.899.5416

**Sacramento**
Rumpelstiltskin
1021 R Street
☎ 916.442.9225

**San Anselmo**
Atelier Marin
217 San Anselmo Avenue
☎ 415.256.9618

**San Diego**
The Grove at Juniper & 30th
3010 Juniper Street
☎ 619.284.7684

Needlecraft Cottage
870 Grand Avenue
☎ 858.272.8185

**San Francisco**
Atelier Yarns
1945 Divisadero Street
☎ 415.771.1550

Carolina Homespun
455 Lisbon Street
☎ 415.584.7786

Greenwich Yarn
2073 Greenwich Street
☎ 415.567.2535

Imagiknit
3897 18th Street
☎ 415.621.6642

**San Jose**
Green Planet Yarn
1702 Meredian Avenue
☎ 408.871.9196

The Knitting Room
1195 Branham Lane
☎ 408.264.7229

**San Luis Obispo**
Nordic Mart
1229A Carmel Street
☎ 805.542.9303

Yarns at the Adobe
964 Chorro Street
☎ 805.549.9276

**San Marcos**
Yarning for You
1001 W. San Marcos Boulevard
Ste.180
☎ 760.744.5648

**San Marino**
A Stitch in Time
2465 Huntington Drive
☎ 626.793.5217

**San Mateo**
Nine Rubies Knitting
28 E. 3rd Avenue, #100
☎ 650.685.6205

**San Rafael**
Come to the Point
10 California Avenue
☎ 415.485.4942

Dharma Trading Company
1604 4th Street
☎ 415.456.1211

**Santa Ana**
Ursula's Yarn Boutique
2441 N. Tustin Avenue
Suite D
☎ 714.834.1908

**Santa Barbara**
Cardigans
3030 State Street
☎ 805.569.0531

Knit Fit
320 W. Carillo Street
☎ 805.963.2331

Loop and Leaf
536 Brinkerhoff Avenue
☎ 805.845.4696

**Santa Clara**
Exclamation Point
1055 Monroe Street
☎ 408.246.3800

**Santa Clarita**
Creative U Studios
17733 Sierra Highway
☎ 661.250.4600

**Santa Cruz**
The Golden Fleece
317 Potrero Street
Ste. D
☎ 831.426.1425

Hart's Fabric
1620 Seabright Avenue
☎ 831.423.5434

The Swift Stitch
402 Ingalls Street, #12
☎ 831.427.9276

**Santa Monica**
Compatto Yarn Salon
2112 Wilshire Boulevard
☎ 310.453.2130

Wildfiber
1453 14th Street, Suite E.
☎ 310.458.2748

**Santa Rosa**
Cast Away
111 4th Street
☎ 707.546.9276

Village Sewing Center
210 Coddington Center
☎ 707.544.7529

**Sausalito**
Bluebird Yarn and Fiber Crafts
325 Pine Street
☎ 415.331.9276

**Sebastopol**
Balls and Skeins
899 Gravenstein Highway S.
Suite C
☎ 707.824.8991

Yarnitudes
3598 Gravenstein Highway S.
☎ 707.827.3618

**Solvang**
Knit fit
1582 Copenhagen
☎ 805.688.0686

Solvang needlework
1578 Mission Drive
☎ 805.688.6151

**Sonora**
By Hand Yarn
106 S. Washington Street
☎ 209.694.8161

**St. Helena**
Muse
1309 Main Street
Suite B
☎ 707.967.9500

**Studio City**
La Knitterie Parisienne
12642 Ventura Boulevard
☎ 818.766.1515

**Sunnyvale**
Purlescence Yarns
564 S. Murphy Avenue
☎ 408.735.9276

**Temecula**
The Wool Lady
28690 Old Town Front Street
Suite 310- Butterfield Plaza
☎ 951.699.2900

**Toluca Lake**
Sit N Stitch
10154 Riverside Drive
☎ 818.760.9330

**Torrance**
Concepts in Yarn and
Needlepoint
24520 Hawthorne Boulevard
☎ 310.791.3800

**Ukiah**
Heidi's Yarn Haven
180 S. School Street
☎ 707.462.0544

**Upland**
Needles and Niceties
1655 N. Mountain Avenue
Suite 116
☎ 909.985.6264

**Valley Village**
Stitch Café
12443 Magnolia Boulevard
☎ 818.980.1234

**Van Nuys**
A-Major-Knitwork
6746 Balboa Boulevard
☎ 818.787.2659

**Venice**
Discoteca La Princesa
834 Lincoln Boulevard
☎ 310.399.9455

**Ventura**
Anacapa Fine Yarns
4572 Telephone Road
Suite 909
☎ 805.654.9500

Fabric Town USA
2686 E. Main Street
☎ 805.643.3434

**Visalia**
Creekside yarns
208 W. Main Street
Suite 10
☎ 559.733.9276

**Walnut Creek**
Fashion Knit
Ygnacio Valley Road
Suite B102
☎ 925.943.3994

**Weaverville**
Sweet Sheep
515 Main Street
☎ 530.623.8650

**Wheatland**
Needles and Hoops
3811 Monarch Trail
☎ 530.301.3154

**Whittier**
The Yarn Garden
7648 Painter Avenue
Suite B
☎ 562.698.1593

**Yorba Linda**
Velona Needlecraft
22435 La Palma Avenue #A
☎ 714.692.2286

# Colorado

**Arvada**
Knit knack
7505-A Grandview Avenue
☎ 303.456.2021

**Aspen**
Aspen Yarn Gallery
520 E. Cooper Avenue #205
☎ 970.925.5667

## Bayfield
Knit One Pearl Street
498 Church Street
☎ 970.884.9008

## Boulder
Gypsy Wools
3216 Arapahoe Avenue
☎ 303.442.1884

Shuttles, Spindles & Skeins
635 S. Broadway, Unit E
☎ 303.494.1071

## Brighton
Deer Pants
121 N. Main Street
☎ 303.654.0882

## Buena Vista
Serendipity Yarn and Gifts
321 West Main Street
☎ 719.395.3110

## Castle Rock
Everything Alpaca
313 3rd Street
☎ 303.660.6684

Stash
360 Perry Street
☎ 303.660.YARN

## Centennial
Colorful Yarns
2001 E. Easter Avenue #101
☎ 303.798.2299

## Colorado Springs
Green Valley Weavers & Knitters
2115 W. Colorado Avenue
☎ 719.448.9963

Needleworks By Holly Berry
2409 W. Colorado Avenue
☎ 719.636.1002

Table Rock Llamas
Fiber Arts Studio
6520 Shoup Road
☎ 719.495.7747

Woolly Works Knit Shop
9 E. Bijou Street
☎ 719.661.6062

The Yarn Outlet
416 S. 8th Street
☎ 719.227.3665

## Conifer
Knit Knook
10903 US Highway285
☎ 303.838.2118

## Denver
Fabric Bliss
828 Santa Fe Drive
☎ 303.893.7922

LambShoppe
3512 E. 12th Avenue
☎ 303.322.2223

I Love Knitting
600 S. Holly Street
Unit 102
☎ 303.399.5648

Tea for Ewe
4234 Tennyson Street
☎ 303.955.4022

**Durango**
Yarn Durango
755 E. Second Avenue
☎ 970.259.9827

**Eagle**
Alpaca
106 Broadway Street
☎ 970.328.1211

**Elbert**
Wooly Works Knit Shop
12285 Oregon Wagon Trail
☎ 719.495.2754

**Englewood**
Wooden Spools
2805 S. Broadway
☎ 303.761.9231

**Estes Park**
Neota Designs Weaving and Yarn Studio
156 Wiest Drive
☎ 970.586.8800

The Stitchin' Den
165 Virginia Drive
☎ 970.577.8210

**Evergreen**
Tall Yarns
4602 Plettner Lane, 1-A
☎ 303.670.1444

YarnWest
3731 Evergreen Parkway
☎ 303.674.6001

**Frisco**
What's Needling U
279 Main Street
☎ 970.668.0381

**Ft. Collins**
The Loopy Ewe
2720 Council Tree Avenue #255
☎ 888.527.9181

Lambspun of Colorado
1101 Lincoln Avenue
☎ 970.484.1998

My Sister Knits
1408 W. Mountain Avenue
☎ 970.407.1461

Your Daily Fiber
325 E. Mulberry Street
☎ 970.484.2414

**Georgetown**
The Quilted Purl
600 Rose Street
☎ 303.569.1115

**Golden**
The Recycled Lamb
2081 Youngfield Street
☎ 303.234.9337

**Granby**
Lonesome Stone Fiber Mill
946 Country Road 60
☎ 970.887.9591

## Grand Junction
The Yarn Store
Orchard Mesa Plaza
2692 Highway 50
Suite J
☎ 970.241.5080

## Greeley
Country Crafts
2200 Reservoir Road
☎ 970.353.1774

Sew Downtown
824 9th Street
☎ 970.352.9230

## Lafayette
Mew Mew's Yarn Shop
2700 Dagny Way
Suite 108
☎ 303.665.5591

## Lakewood
Showers of Flowers Yarn
6900 West Colfax Avenue
☎ 303.233.2525

## Lamar
Crafters Corner
122 S. Main Street
☎ 719.336.0318

## Larkspur
Larkspur Funny Farm
and Fiber Studio
10209 East Jones Road
☎ 303.814.0047

## Leadville
Fire on the Mountain
715 Harrison Avenue
☎ 719.486.2071

## Littleton
A Knitted Peace
5654C Prince Street
☎ 303.730.0366

## Longmont
Longmont Yarn Shop
454 Main Street
☎ 303.678.8242

Nature's Own Imagination
7128 Mt. Meeker Road
☎ 303.530.5049

## Monte Vista
Shades, Quilts & Etc.
129 Adams Street
☎ 719.852.2179

## Nederland
The Alpaca Store...and More
30 W. Boulder Street
☎ 303.258.1400

## Pagosa Springs
Eagle Mountain Mercantile
56 Talisman Drive 8C
☎ 970.731.9900

## Paonia
Delicious Orchards
39126 Highway 133
☎ 970.527.1110

**Salida**
Fringe
139 F Street
☎ 719.539.4006

**Steamboat Springs**
The Fiber Exchange
624 Lincoln Avenue
#102
☎ 970.879.9090

Knitch
1910 Ski Time Square
#102
☎ 970.871.6675

Sew Steamboat
929 Lincoln Avenue
☎ 970.879.3222

**Sterling**
FiberSpace
113 N. 2nd Street
☎ 970.521.9041

**Telluride**
Needle Rock Fiberarts
320 W. Colorado Avenue
☎ 970.728.3427

**Walsenburg**
Edla's Yarns
302 W. 7th Street
☎ 719.738.3318

**Woodland Park**
Nikki's Knots
301 US Highway 24
☎ 719.686.6424

Nuts 'n Bolts Needlworks
200 S. Chestnut Street
☎ 719.687.2272

**Wray**
You Keep Me in Stitches
301 S. Main Street
☎ 970.332.5556

# Connecticut

**Avon**
Knit & Pearls
395 W. Avon Road
☎ 860.404.0694

Village Needlecrafts
19 E. Main Street
☎ 860.678.1882

Yarnover
124 Simsbury Road
☎ 860.404.5375

**Bethel**
A Stitch in Time
276 Greenwood Avenue
☎ 203.748.1002

**Bozrah**
Mothers of Purl Yarn
441 Salem Turnpike
☎ 860.823.0434

Six Paca Boutique & Brew
44 Bozrah Street
☎ 860.204.0386

**Branford**
The Yarn Basket
288 E. Main Street
☎ 203.208.3288

**Bristol**
New England Yarn & Spindle
801 Terryville Avenue
☎ 860.516.4646

**Canterbury**
Burgis Brook Alpacas
44 N. Canterbury Road
☎ 860.546.6828

**Chaplin**
Yarns with a Twist
111 Willimantic Road/ Rte 6
☎ 860.455.9986

**Colchester**
Colchester Mill Fabrics
120 Lebanon Avenue
☎ 860.537.2004

**Deep River**
Yarns Down Under
37C Hillside Terrace
☎ 860.526.9986

**Eastford**
Still River Mill
210 Eastford Road
☎ 860.974.9918

**Glastonbury**
Village Wool
2279 Main Street
☎ 860.633.0898

**Grandby**
Marji's Yarncrafts
381 Salmon Brook Street
☎ 860.653.9700

**Haddam**
CT Yarn & Wool Company
85 Bridge Road
☎ 860.345.9300

Woolie Bullies
396 Saybrook Road
☎ 860.345.1008

**Kent**
Black Sheep Yarns
12 Old Barn Road
☎ 860.927.3808

**Madison**
Madison Wool
56- A Wall Street
☎ 203.245.5921

**Marlborough**
The Yarn Garden
47 N. Main Street
☎ 203.237.6446

**Middletown**
Pamela Roose Hand-Knits
& Yarn
88 Court Street
☎ 860.788.2715

**Mystic River**
Driftwood Yarns
29 1/2 Broadway Avenue
☎ 860.415.8118

Mystic River Yarns
14 Holmes Street
☎ 860.536.4305

**New Haven**
Knit New Haven
26 Whitney Avenue
☎ 203.777.5648

**Newtown**
The Sheep Shoppe
136A Mount Pleasant Road
☎ 203.364 5600

**New London**
Dagmar's Yarn Shop
80 Montauk Avenue
☎ 860.442.8364

**Old Saybrook**
Saybrook Yarn
99 Main Street
☎ 860.388.3415

**Plainville**
Bayberry Knitting
36 Whiting Street #1
☎ 860.410.4250

**Putnam**
Woodworks
154 Main Street
☎ 860.963.1228

**Ridgefield**
Nancy O
23 Katonah Street
☎ 203.431.2266

**Somers**
Knitting Creations
12 South Road
☎ 860.749.4005

**Vernon**
Knit Two-Gether
435 K Hartford Turnpike
☎ 860.870.3883

**Wallingford**
Country Yarn
9 S. Colony Road
☎ 203.269.6662

**Westfield**
Westfield Yarn & Thread Studio
22 School Street
☎ 413.568.8384

**Windsor**
Creative Fibers
645 Poquonock Avenue
☎ 860.687.9931

**Woodbridge**
The Yarn Barn
1666 Litchfield Turnpike
☎ 203.389.5117

# Delaware

**Bethany Beach**
Sea Needles
780 Garfield Parkway
☎ 302.539.0574

**Dagsboro**
Serendipity Quilt Shop
31821 Cannon Street
☎ 302.732.6304

**Lewes**
Ginger Moon - Fine Yarn
& Antiques
107 B Market Street
☎ 302.644.2970

**Newark**
Stitches with Style
16 E. Polly Drummond
Shopping Center
☎ 203.453.8130

**Rehoboth Beach**
Kitschy Stitch
413 Rehoboth Avenue
☎ 302.260.9138

# District of Columbia

Looped Yarn Works
1732 Connecticut Avenue NW
#200
☎ 202.714.5667

# Florida

**Altamonte Springs**
Knitting Patch
Westmonte Plaza, Suite 1108
195 S. Westmonte Drive
☎ 407.331.5648

**Apalachicola**
Downtown Books & Purl
67 Commerce Street
☎ 850.653.1290

**Belleair Bluffs**
The Flying Needle
432 Indian Rocks Road N.
☎ 727.581.8691

**Boca Raton**
The Knit Shoppe
9070 Kimberly Boulevard
Suite 48
☎ 561.488.4377

**Brandon**
Brandon Yarn Boutique
211 S. Moon Avenue
☎ 813.409.3859

**Bunnell**
Sew & Quilt Shop
4601 E. Moody Boulevard
☎ 386.586.5409

**Cocoa**
Knit and Stich
15 Stone Street
☎ 321.632.4579

**Coral Gables**
Giving Tree
248 Giralda Avenue
☎ 305.445.3867

The Knitting Garden
1923 Ponce de Leon Blvd
☎ 305.774.1060

**Delray Beach**
Knitters Nook
5195 W. Atlantic Avenue
Suites J & K
☎ 561.495.1095

Stitches by the Sea
710 E. Atlantic Avenue
☎ 561.865.5775

**Dunedin**
Raspberries
728 Douglas Avenue
☎ 727.738.1477

**Dunnellon**
Stitch Niche
20782 Walnut Street
☎ 352.465.8000

**Ft. Lauderdale**
Once Upon A Quilt
3404 Griffin Road
☎ 954.987.8827

Yarns and Arts
3330 NE 32nd Street
☎ 954.990.5772

**Ft. Myers**
Geez Leweez
16876 McGregor Boulevard
☎ 239.395.2900

**Ft. White**
Bella Luna Knits
18387 SW State Road
☎ 386.497.1433

**Gainesville**
Yarnworks
4113 NW 13th Street
☎ 352.337.9965

**Havana**
Cindy's Needlework Cottage
1210 Collins Road
☎ 850.539.7201

**Homosassa**
Fiber Odyssey
6410 S. Suncoast Boulevard
☎ 352.628.9276

**Jacksonville**
Knitwitz
9545 San Jose Boulevard
☎ 904.260.1636

A Stitch in Time
5724 St. Augustine Road
☎ 904.731.4082

**Jupiter**
Knit Or Knot
1432 S. Cypress Drive
☎ 561.746.1005

**Kissimmee**
Needle Craft World
4151 W. Vine Street
☎ 407.933.5955

**Lake Worth**
Just Imaginknit
6663 Lake Worth Rd #B
☎ 561.433.3444

**Largo**
Criativity
720 9th Avenue SW
☎ 727.584.4191

**Longwood**
Knit!
900 Fox Valley Drive
Suite 106
☎ 407.767.5648

**Maitland**
Sip & Knit, Inc.
9400 S. Highway 17-92
Suite 1016
☎ 407.622.5648

**Miami**
Elegant Stitches
8841 SW 132nd Street
☎ 305.232.4005

**Milton**
Yarns & Things
5211 Dogwood Drive
☎ 850.382.4670

**Miramar Beach**
Destin Yarn Shop
12273 US Highway 98 W.
Unit 109
☎ 850.650.0006

**Naples**
Knitting with Nancy
3804 Tamiami Trail E.
☎ 239.793.8141

**North Palm Beach**
Needlepoint Alley
1201 US Highway 1, #18
☎ 561.691.3223

**Ocala**
Yards 'N Yarn
1913 NE 14th Street
☎ 352.351.6110

**Odessa**
Fiber Art
8727 Gunn Highway
☎ 813.792.5999

**Orlando**
The Black Sheep
1322 N. Mills Avenue
☎ 407.644.0122

**Ormond Beach**
Ball of Yarn
156-A W. Granada Boulevard
☎ 386.672.2858

**Pembroke Pines**
Raging Wool
1850 NW 122 Terrace
☎ 954.385.0861

**Pensacola**
A & E. Fabric & Craft
923 N. New Warrington Road
☎ 850.455.0112

Kings Sewing and Knitting
2633 Creighton Road
☎ 850.476.2660

**Plantation**
A Stitcher's Haven
10055 Cleary Boulevard
☎ 954.476.3788

**Saint Petersburg**
Stitchworm
5277 Park Street N.
☎ 727.541.6571

**Sarasota**
Eye of the Needle
1817 South Osprey Avenue
☎ 941.955.0458

A Good Yarn
7418 S. Tamiami Trail
☎ 941.487.7914

Picasso's Moon Yarn Shop
200 S. Washington Boulevard
☎ 941.932.0103

**Silver Springs**
E.T. Yarns
5300 Silver Springs Boulevard
☎ 352.236.3000

**Summerfield**
The Yarn Lady
16810 S. US Highway 441
Suite 501
☎ 352.693.2065

**Tallahassee**
Really Knit Stuff
565 Industrial Drive
☎ 850.907.3590

Yarn Therapy
1760 Thomasville Road
☎ 850.577.0555

**Tampa**
Knit 'n Knibble
4027 S. Dale Mabry Highway
☎ 813.837.5648

**Tarpon Springs**
Mamma Lane's Coffee
212 E. Tarpon Avenue
☎ 727.934.5120

**Venice**
Knit N. Stitch Shop
5115 State Road 776
☎ 941.408.7416

Knitting Place
258 Miami Avenue W.
☎ 941.486.1584

**Vero Beach**
Four Purls
331 3rd Street NW
☎ 863.662.8288

The Knitty Gritty
1561 Old Dixie Highway
Suite B
☎ 772.778.9199

**Winter Haven**
Four Purls
334 3rd Street NW
☎ 863.662.8288

# Georgia

**Acworth**
Yarn & Stuff
4442 S. Main Street
☎ 770.575.2152

**Alpharetta**
Only Ewe and Cotton Too
12315 Crabapple Road
Suite 152
☎ 770.740.0844

**Athens**
Revival Yarns
297 Prince Avenue
Suite 19
☎ 706.850.1354

**Atlanta**
Needle Nook
2165 Briarcliff Road
☎ 404.325.0068

Yarning for Ewe
3220 Cobb Parkway
Suite 102
☎ 678.909.4963

**Canton**
Knitting in the Red Yarn Shop
2864 E. Cherokee Drive
Suite D
☎ 770.402.9610

**Carrollton**
Ewe Knit and Crochet
815 Cedar Street
☎ 770.830.6480

**Cartersville**
The King's Knit-Wit
12 S. Wall Street
☎ 770.883.9023

**Clarkesville**
Bumble berry Yarn
1345 Washington Street
☎ 706.754.0462

**Cumming**
Fleece
1735 Buford Highway
Suite 210
☎ 770.886.5648

**Dahlonega**
Magical Threads
315 Church Street
☎ 706.867.8918

**Decatur**
Sheepish
308 W. Ponce de Leon Avenue
Suite F2
☎ 404.377.6875

**Duluth**
Rare Purls Yarn Boutique
3579 W. Lawrenceville Street
☎ 770.910.7626

**Ellijay**
Strings & Stitches Yarn Shoppe
449 Industrial Boulevard #165
☎ 706.698.5648

**Gainesville**
Yarn Rhapsody
475 Dawsonville Highway
Suite C
☎ 770.536.3130

**Garden City**
Sew Much More
4831 Augusta Road
Suite A
☎ 912.966.5626

**Hahira**
Rabbit Moon Yarn
107 W. Main Street
☎ 229.794.8162

**Hartwell**
ElsieBee Originals
79 Depot Street
☎ 706.376.2787

**Hinesville**
Candra's Yarn Paradise
114 S. Commerce Street
☎ 912.200.7859

**Hoschton**
Yarn Junkees
25 City Square
☎ 706.921.4116

**Lawrenceville**
Yarn Garden
159 W. Pike Street
☎ 678.225.0920

**Macon**
Creative Yarns
134 Speer Avenue
☎ 478.746.5648

**Madison**
Sartoria Monica
232 W. Washington Street
☎ 706.343.0000

**Marietta**
Lovin' Knit Studio
255 Village Parkway NE
Suite 610
☎ 770.612.5648

**Peachtree City**
Sugarfoot Yarns
100 N. Peachtree Parkway
☎ 770.487.9001

**Roswell**
Cast-On Cottage and
Needlepoint Garden
Coleman Village
860 Marietta Highway
☎ 770.998.3483

**Savannah**
The Frayed Knot
6 W. State Street
☎ 912.233.1240

Unwind Yarn & Gifts
7710 Waters Avenue
☎ 912.303.3970

Wild Fibre
6 E. Liberty Street
☎ 912.238.0514

**St. Simons Island**
The Stitchery of St. Simons
3411 Frederica Road
☎ 912.638.3401

**Smyrna**
Eat-Sleep-Knit
6400 Highlands Parkway
Suite 1
☎ 770.432.9277

**Thomasville**
Fuzzy Goat
223 W. Jackson Street
☎ 229.236.4628

**Watkinsville**
The Yarn House
2411 Hog Mountain Road
☎ 706.705.1720

**Woodstock**
The Whole Nine Yarns
8826 Main Street
☎ 678.494.5242

# Hawaii

**Hanalei**
Strings and Things
5-5190 Kuhio Highway
☎ 808.826.9633

**Hilo**
Big Island Bernina Yarn Basket
50 E. Puainako Street
Suite 107
☎ 808.959.0034

Yarn Basket
50 E. Puainako Street
☎ 808.959.0034

**Honokowai**
Binky's Hawaii
3600 Lower Honoapiilani Road
☎ 808.276.7474

**Honolulu**
Isle Knit
1188 Bishop Street
Suite 1416
☎ 808.533.0853

Yarn Story
1411 S. King Street
#201
☎ 808.593.2212

**Kailua**
Yarn & Needlecrafts
46 Hoolai Street
☎ 808.262.9555

**Kailua Kona**
Island Yarn and Art Supplies
73-5568 Olowalu Street
☎ 808.326.2820

Quilt Passions
75-5626 Kuakini Highway
Suite 4
☎ 808.329.7475

**Kaneohe**
Aloha Yarn
46-018 Kamehameha Highway
☎ 808.234.5865

**Kihei**
The Maui Quilt Shop
Zeka Shopping Center - Makai
1280 S. Kihei Road
☎ 808.874.8050

# Idaho

**Boise**
Knit Wits
12668 W. Fairview Avenue
☎ 208.376.0040

Twisted Ewe
1738 W. State Street
☎ 208.287.3693

**Coeur d'Alene**
Knit-n-Crochet
600 W. Kathleen Avenue
Suite 30
☎ 208.676.9276

**Grangeville**
Home Grown Quilts
207 W. Main Street
☎ 208.983.0254

**Idaho Falls**
Madsen's Crafts and Framing
2125 W. Broadway Street
☎ 208.523.6074

Yarn Connection
415 Park Avenue
☎ 208.524.8256

**Ketchum**
Sun Valley Needle Arts
351 Leadville Avenue N.
☎ 208.928.7620

**Kimberly**
The Quilt Barn
241 Main Street N.
☎ 208.423.5092

**McCall**
Keep Me In Stitches
136 E. Lake Street
☎ 208.634.2906

**Moscow**
The Yarn Underground
409 S. Washington Street
☎ 208.882.7700

**Meridian**
Puffy Mondaes
200 12th Ave S.
☎ 208.407.3359

**Orofino**
Wild Hare
222 Johnson Avenue
☎ 208.476.3358

**Payette**
Cat's Crochet Corner
33 S. Main Street
☎ 208.642.1155

**Pocatello**
Mustard Seed Dreams
362 N. Main Street
☎ 208.478.2688

**Rexburg**
Porter's Craft & Frame
19 College Avenue
☎ 208.359.0786

Twisting Fibers
22 Carlson Avenue
☎ 208.709.5448

**Rigby**
Abbotts Variety
120 E. Main Street
☎ 208.745.7738

**Sandpoint**
A Child's Dream
214 Cedar Street
Suite A
☎ 208.255.1664

Something Olde Something New
504 Oak Street
☎ 208.263.9447

**Shelley**
The Ribbon Retreat
650 N. State Street
☎ 208.357.3887

# Illinois

**Barrington**
Gene Ann's Yarns
117 E. Station Street
☎ 847.842.9321

**Big Rock**
Esther's Place
201 US 30
☎ 630.556.9665

**Bloomington**
Mary Lynn's Yarn Garden
318 N. Main Street
☎ 309.820.0174

Treadle II
2101 Eastland Drive
☎ 309.662.1733

Village Stitches
901 S. Eldorado Road
☎ 309.663.9031

**Buffalo Grove**
Knit Happens
794 S. Buffalo Grove Road
☎ 847.340.7701

**Casey**
The Yarn Studio
2 E. Main Street
☎ 217.932.5851

**Champaign**
Needleworks
24 E. Green #5
☎ 217.352.1340

**Chicago**
Knit1
3823 N. Lincoln Ave
☎ 773.244.1646

Loopy Yarns
47 W. Polk Street
☎ 312.583.9276

Nina
1655 W. Division Street
☎ 773.486.8996

Sifu Design Studio & Fine Yarns
6054 N. Broadway Street
☎ 773.271.7438

Sister ARTS Studio
721 W. Wrightwood Avenue
☎ 773.929.7274

We'll Keep You in Stitches
67 E. Oak Street
☎ 312.642.2540

Windy Knitty
5653 N. Clark Street
☎ 773.800.9276

The Woolly Lamb Yarn Studio
6007 N. Nina Avenue
☎ 773.631.6208

**Crystal Lake**
Sunflower Samplings
89 N. Williams Street
☎ 815.455.2919

**Danville**
Needleworks
207 S. Buchanan
☎ 217.213.5459

**Downers Grove**
Knitche
5221 Main Street
☎ 630.852.5648

**Dunlap**
Knit 4 Together Yarn Co.
209 N. Second Street
☎ 309.243.9499

**Elgin**
Elgin Knit Works
8 Douglas Avenue
☎ 847.627.4700

**Elmhurst**
The Knitting Pot
111 E. First Street, #107
☎ 630.561.3186

**Evanston**
CloseKnit
531 Davis Street
☎ 847.328.6760

Montoya Fiber Studio
2566 Prairie Avenue
☎ 847.869.1089

**Fairview Heights**
The Bead Place
5200 N. Illinois Street
☎ 618.222.0772

**Forest Park**
Knit Nirvana
7453 Madison Street
☎ 708.771.5232

**Frankfort**
Yarns to Dye For
19 Ash Street
☎ 815.469.4906

**Freeport**
Wall of Yarn
14 W. Stephenson Street
☎ 815.616.8402

**Galena**
Fiber Wild
304 S. Main Street
☎ 815.777.3550

**Galesburg**
Knit 102
31 N. Kellogg Street
☎ 309.343.0965

**Glen Ellyn**
String Theory Yarn Co.
477 North Main
☎ 630.469.6085

**Highland Park**
Magic Needle
463 Roger Williams Avenue
☎ 847.432.9897

Mia Bella Yarn & Accessories
1815 St. Johns Avenue
☎ 847.748.8419

**Knoxville**
Sit-n-Knit Yarn Shop
236 E. Main Street
☎ 309.289.2379

**LaGrange**
Idea Studio
515 S. La Grange Road
☎ 708.352.1789

**Lincoln**
Serendipity Stitches
129 S. Kickapoo
☎ 217.732.8811

**Lisle**
The Nook
4738 Main Street
☎ 630.968.0764

**Lockport**
Betsy's Yarn & Tea Shop
201 W. 10th Street
☎ 815.836.0470

**Loves Park**
The Wool Gathering
6156 E. Riverside Boulevard
☎ 815.637.9666

**Macomb**
Studio III Stitchery
129 S. Randolf
☎ 309.837.4558

**Marengo**
The Fold
3316 Millstream Road
☎ 815.568.5320

**Maroa**
Country Lace & Wood Creations
111 W. Main Street
☎ 217.794.5048

**Milan**
Naked Sheep Yarn Barn
208 4th Street W.
☎ 309.283.7167

**Morris**
Le Mouton Rouge Knittery
407 Liberty Street
☎ 815.941.9100

**Mt. Prospect**
Mosaic Yarn Studio
109 W. Prospect Avenue
☎ 847.390.1013

**Naperville**
Gentler Times Stitching
124 S. Webster Street
Suite 102
☎ 630.637.0680

**Nauvoo**
Art Needlework Shop
1265 Mulholland Street
☎ 217.453.6769

**Northbrook**
Three Bags Full Knitting Studio
1927 Cherry Lane
☎ 847.291.9933

**Oak Park**
Knot Just Knits
1109 Westgate Street
☎ 708.948.7943

**Oregon**
Stitches in Time
300 Washington Street
☎ 815.732.4599

**Orland Park**
Knitting Etc.
14428 John Humphrey Drive
☎ 708.349.7941

**Peoria**
The Fiber Universe
305 SW Water Street
Unit 1A
☎ 309.673.5659

**Princeton**
Quilter's Garden
527 S. Main Street
☎ 815.879.3739

**Quincy**
Knit Your Dreams
635 N. 66th Street
☎ 217.222.3335

**Richmond**
Wool, Warp & Wheel
5605 Mill Street
☎ 815.678.4063

**Saint Charles**
Wool and Company
107A W. Main Street
☎ 630.232.2305

Fine Line Creative Arts Center
6N 158 Crane Road
☎ 630.584.9443

**Shelbyville**
Main Street Quilt Company
200 E. Main Street
☎ 217.774.3484

**Shorewood**
Elemental Yarns
720 Cottage Street
☎ 815.729.7410

**Springfield**
Nanncy's Knitworks
1305 Wabash Avenue
☎ 217.546.0600

Knit Wits
2205 Wabash Avenue
#103
☎ 217.698.6100

**St. Herrin**
The Yarn Shoppe
105 N. 16th
☎ 618.988.9276

**Urbana**
Klose Knit
311 W. Springfield
☎ 217.344.2123

**Westmont**
TLD Design Center & Gallery
26 E. Quincy Street
☎ 630.963.9573

**Westville**
Cooke's Craft Cottage
11 Lyons Road
☎ 217.267.2088

**Wheaton**
Craftique Never Enough Knitting
121 N. Main Street
☎ 630.221.1007

Lizzie's Yarn
300 S. Main Street
☎ 630.690.7945

# Indiana

**Angola**
The Yarnery
116 N. Public Square
☎ 260.316.5551

**Arcadia**
Tabby Tree Weaver
107 E. Main Street
☎ 317.984.5475

**Aurora**
Distinctive Knits
322 Second Street
☎ 812.926.2970

**Bloomington**
In A Yarn Basket
1907 S. Walnut Street
Smith Shoe Center
☎ 812.330.5394

Yarns Unlimited
115 S. Walnut Street
Suite A
☎ 812.334.2464

**Columbus**
Homestead Weaving Studio
6285 S. Hamilton Creek Road
☎ 812.988.8622

Knitters Nook
3623 25th Street
☎ 812.657.7669

Shabby Sheep & Ewe
1113 16th Street
☎ 812.372.9276

**Dale**
Shirley's Sewing Stuff
11356 S. US 231
Between Dale and Huntingburg
☎ 812.683.3377

**Evansville**
Knitwitts Yarn Shoppe
A6219 Vogel Road #101
☎ 812.471.8540

**Fairmount**
Knit 'n' Purl
5480 W. 1100 S.
☎ 765.551.7875

**Ferdinand**
3 Bags Full
Ferdinand Antique Emporium
1440 Main Street
☎ 812.639.7277

**Ft. Wayne**
Knitting Off Broadway
1309 Broadway
☎ 260.422.9276

**Goshen**
Reverie, Yarn, Gifts and Décor
111 E. Washington Street
☎ 574.971.5129

**Greenfield**
Zig-Zag Corner Quilts & Baskets
7872 N. Troy Road
☎ 317.326.3115

**Indianapolis**
Mass Ave Knit Shop
862 Virginia Avenue
☎ 317.638.1833

**Jeffersonville**
Grinny Possum Fiber Arts
326 Spring Street
☎ 812.284.9400

**Kokomo**
Khadija Knit Shop
3712 S. Lafountain Street
☎ 765.453.4652

**Lafayette**
River Knits
846 Main Street
☎ 765.742.5648

**Laotto**
Wolley Knob Fiber Mill
207 S. Main Street
☎ 260.897.4477

**Madison**
Fabric shop
220 E. Main Street
☎ 812.265.5828

Harriette's Knit Knook
103 E. Main Street
☎ 812.274.2040

**Martinsville**
Sheep Street Fibers
6535 SR 252
☎ 812.597.5648

**Nashville**
The Clay Purl
58 E. Main
Suite 3
☎ 812.988.0336

**Noblesville**
Always In Stitches
1808 Conner Street
☎ 317.776.4227

Black Sheep Yarn and Fiber Arts
1095 E. Conner Street
☎ 317.900.7117

**New Carlisle**
Yarn and More
106 S. Filbert Street
☎ 574.654.3300

**Noblesville**
Always In Stitches
1808 E. Conner Street
☎ 317.776.4227

**Pendleton**
The Trading Post for Fiber Arts
8833 Knightstown Road
☎ 765.778.3331

**Peru**
Knit Knack Shop
3378 W. 550 N.
☎ 765.985.3164

**Plainfield**
Nomad Yarns
218 E. Main Street
☎ 317.742.7456

**Plymouth**
The Yarn Loft
214 W. Washington Street
☎ 574.935.9276

**Richmond**
Ply Fiber Arts
921 E. Main Street
☎ 765.966.5648

**Rockville**
Fiber Closet
120 S. Market Street
☎ 765.569.2953

**Shelbyville**
Scotland Yarn
13 Public Square
☎ 317.398.9276

**Shipshewana**
D'Vine Gallery
310 N. Harrison Street
☎ 260.768.7110

**South Bend**
Erica's Craft & Sewing Center
1320 N. Ironwood Drive
☎ 574.233.3112

Heckaman's Quilting & Yarn
63028 U.S.31 S.
☎ 574.291.3918

**Street Joe**
The Big Red Barn
6205 State Road 1
☎ 260.446.7997

**Terre Haute**
River Wools
671 Wabash Avenue
☎ 812.238.0090

**Valparaiso**
Sheep's Clothing
60 W. Lincolnway
☎ 219.462.1700

**Vincennes**
Atkinson Farm
1061 Atkinson Road
☎ 812.726.1306

**Zionsville**
Village Yarn Shop
209 S. Main Street
☎ 317.873.0004

# Iowa

**Ames**
The Rose Tree Fiber Shop
2814 West Street
☎ 515.292.7076

**Ankeny**
Knitting Next Door
704 SW Third Street
☎ 515.963.0396

**Bettendorf**
Knit and Knot
3359 Devils Glen Road
☎ 563.332.7378

**Cantril**
Dutchman's Store
103 Division Street
☎ 319.397.2322

**Carroll**
Yarn Basket
512 N. Adams Street
☎ 712.792.2890

**Charles City**
Stitches
715 Kelly Mall
☎ 641.228.3383

**Davenport**
The Yarn Shoppe
903 E. Kimberly Road
Suite 20
☎ 563.359.1002

**Decorah**
Blue Heron Knittery
300 W. Water Street
☎ 563.517.105

**Des Moines**
Hill Vintage and Knits
432 East Locust
☎ 515.288.2287

Yarn Junction
132 5th Street W.
☎ 515.277.2770

**Dubuque**
Yarn Soup
1005 Main Street
☎ 563.587.8044

**Fairfield**
At Home Store
52 N. Main Street
☎ 641.472.1016

**Independence**
Stitcher's Hideaway
115 1st Street E.
☎ 319.332.1076

**Iowa City**
Home Ec. Workshop
207 N. Linn Street
☎ 319.337.4775

Knitting Shoppe
2141 Muscatine Avenue
☎ 319.337.4920

**Iowa Falls**
Pointy Stix
1707 N. Oak Street
☎ 641.648.3908

**La Motte**
Irish Meadows Yarn Barn & Boutique
23477 Bellevue Cascade Road
☎ 563.543.1375

**Manchester**
The Stitchin Post
112 N. Franklin Street
☎ 563.608.4922

**Marion**
Village Needlework
1127 7th Avenue
☎ 319.362.3271

**Marshalltown**
The Sheep's Stockings
126 W. Main Street
☎ 641.753.4661

**New London**
Country Lane Fiber Arts & Gifts
2860 Quincy Avenue
☎ 319.367.5065

**Tipton**
Fabric Stasher
505 Cedar Street
☎ 563.886.1600

**Urbandale**
Stitch 'n Frame
7611 Douglas Avenue
Suite 21
☎ 515.270.1066

**Waterloo**
Three Oaks Knits
2827 University Avenue
☎ 319.266.6221

**Waverly**
Fiberworks Needlework Shop
108 E. Bremer Avenue
☎ 319.352.5464

**Williamsburg**
Woolen Needle
225 W. Welsh Street
☎ 319.668.2642

**Winterset**
Heartland Fiber Company
112 N. 1st Avenue
☎ 515.468.8593

**Zionsville**
Village Yarn Shop
209 S. Main Street
☎ 317.873.0004

# Kansas

**Abilene**
Shivering Sheep
308 N. Buckeye
☎ 785.263.7501

**Gove**
Gove City Yarns and Buttons
319 Broad Street
☎ 785.938.2255

**Hastings**
The Plum Nelly
734 W. 2nd Street
☎ 402.462.2490

**Hays**
Quilt Cottage
2520 Vine Street
☎ 785.625.0080

## Hutchinson
Yarn
15 E. 14th Street
☎ 620.664.9656

## Lawrence
Yarn Barn
930 Massachusetts Street
☎ 785.842.4333

## Manhattan
Wildflower Yarns & Knitwear
300 Poyntz Avenue
☎ 785.537.1826

## McPherson
Oh Yarn It
221 South Main Street
☎ 620.504.5001

## Newton
The Creation Station
605 N. Main Street
☎ 316.772.0883

## Overland Park
Mystic Knits
6917 West 76th Terrace
☎ 913.396.9609

The Studio Knitting & Needlepoint
9555 Nall Avenue
☎ 816.531.4466

Yarn Shop & More
7212 West 80th Street
☎ 913.649.9276

## Phillipsburg
The Shepherd's Mill
839 Third Street
☎ 785.543.3128

## Salina
Yarns Sold and Told
148 S. Santa Fe Avenue
☎ 785.820.5648

## Topeka
Yak 'n Yarn
5331 SW 22nd Place
☎ 785.272.9276

## Wamego
The Wicked Stitch Yarn & Fiber
523 Lincoln
☎ 785.458.6100

## Wichita
Heritage Hut
2820 E. Douglas Avenue
☎ 316.682.4082

A New Twist
607 W. Douglas Avenue
☎ 316.262.9276

## Winfield
iYarn
915 Main Street
☎ 620.229.8381

# Kentucky

## Ashland
Yarn and More
Kentucky 716
☎ 606.928.1554

**Berea**
Fiber Frenzy
315 Chestnut Street
☎ 859.985.8891

Log House Craft Gallery
200 Estill Street
☎ 859.985.3226

**Bowling Green**
Crafty Hands
2910 Scottsville Road
Suite B
☎ 270.846.4865

**Burlington**
Eagle Bend Alpacas Fiber &Gift Shoppe
7812 East Bend Road
☎ 859.750.3560

**Cadiz**
Red Roof Ranch Alpacas
284 Old Rocky Point Road
☎ 270.206.0367

**Clarkville**
Enchanted Yarn and Fiber
2327 Madison Street
☎ 270.772.1675

**Crescent Springs**
Knitwits Contemporary Yarn Shop
620 Buttermilk Pike
☎ 859.341.2423

**Dry Ridge**
The Quilt Box
490 E. Flynn Road
☎ 859.824.4007

**Elizabethtown**
Blueball Mountain Spindle & Needleworks
308 Central Avenue
☎ 270.763.3352

**Frankfort**
The Woolery
315 Clair Street
☎ 502.352.9800

**Henderson**
Memories Yarn Cafe
324 N. Elm Street
☎ 270.844.0014

**LaGrange**
Friends and Fiber Inc
106 E. Main Street
☎ 502.222.0658

**Lexington**
Magpie Yarn
513 E. High Street
☎ 859.455.7437

ReBelle
225 Rosemont Garden
☎ 859.389.9750

The Stitch Niche
180 Moore Drive
☎ 859.277.2604

**Louisville**
Dee's Crafts
5045 Shelbyville Road
☎ 502.896.6755

Designs in Textiles
1234 S. Third Street
Historic Old Louisville
☎ 502.212.7500

The Little Loomhouse
328 Kenwood Hill Road
☎ 502.367.4792

Sophie's Fine Yarn Shoppe
10482 Shelbyville Road
Suite 101
☎ 502.244.4927

A Yarn Crossing
2123 Frankfort Avenue
☎ 502.822.1315

**Murray**
Red Bug on 3rd
109 N. 3rd Street
☎ 270.761.2723

**Newport**
Knit On!
735 Monmouth Street
☎ 859.291.5648

**Nicholasville**
A Tangled Yarn
605 N. Main Street
☎ 859.608.5419

**Paducah**
With Ewe in Mind
830 Jefferson Street
☎ 270.331.1776

**Russell**
Janis Campbell Knitting Studio
424 Bluebird Drive
☎ 606.494.2301

**Utica**
Special Things
3890 Crane Pond Road
☎ 270.275.9331

**Winchester**
Judy's Stitch in Time
515 West Lexington Avenue
☎ 859.744.7404

# Louisiana

**Baton Rouge**
Knits by Nana
7809 Jefferson Highway
Building E.
☎ 225.572.9872

Weaver's Corner
1586 Cameron Avenue
☎ 225.324.8939

**Hammond**
Tealou & Josephine
219 W. Thomas Street
☎ 985.345.0527

**Lacombe**
McNeedles
28120 Highway 190
☎ 985.882.7144

**Lafayette**
The Yarn Nook
1120B Coolidge Street
☎ 337.593.8558

**New Orleans**
Bette Bornside Co.
2733 Dauphine Street
☎ 504.945.4069

Garden District Needlework Store
2011 Magazine Street
☎ 504.558.0221

Needle Arts Studio
5301 Canal Boulevard
☎ 504.832.3050

Needlework Vault
1927 Sophie Wright Place
☎ 504.528.9797

The Quarter Stitch
629 Chartres Street
☎ 504.522.4451

**Ruston**
Stitchville
120 S. Trenton Street
☎ 318.255.6446

**Shreveport**
Knitting under the Influence
Pierremont Common
6505 Line Avenue #48
☎ 318.866.9984

Yarn on Youree
3622 Youree Drive
☎ 318.210.0670

# Maine

**Auburn**
Quiltessentials
909 Minot Avenue
☎ 207.784.4486

**Bangor**
One Lupine Fiber Arts
170 Park Street
☎ 207.992.4140

The Yarn Barn
849 Stillwater Avenue
☎ 207.922.7989

**Bar Harbor**
Bee's
59 Cottage Street
☎ 207.288.9046

**Bath**
Halcyon Yarn
12 School Street
☎ 800.341.0282

**Belfast**
Good Karma Farm
67 Perkins Road
☎ 207.322.0170

Heavenly Socks Yarns
82 Main Street
☎ 207.338.8388

Nancy's Sewing Center
216 Belmont Avenue
☎ 207.338.1205

**Berwick**
Village Quilt Shop
14 Wilson Street
☎ 207.451.0590

**Blue Hill**
Blue Hill Yarn Shop
176 Ellsworth Road
☎ 207.374.5631

String Theory
132 Beech Hill
☎ 207.374.9990

**Brunswick**
Purl Diva
3 Summer Street
☎ 207.373.0373

**Camden**
The Cashmere Goat
20 Bayview Street
☎ 207.236.7236

**Cumberland**
The Elegant Knitter
at Goose Pond
176 Gray Road
☎ 207.829.2708

**Damariscotta**
Attic Heirlooms
157 Main Street
☎ 207.712.9914

Pine Tree Yarns
74 Main Street
☎ 207.563.5003

**Dixfield**
Log Cabin Craftworks
31 Main Street
☎ 207.562.8816

**Farmingdale**
Hook Yarn & Stitcher
642 Maine Avenue
☎ 207.621.0344

**Farmington**
Pins & Needles
157 Main Street
☎ 207.779.9060

**Freeport**
Casco Bay Fibers
15 Main Street
☎ 207.869.5429

Grace Robinson & Company
208 U.S. Route 1 S.
☎ 207.865.6110

Mother of Purl Yarn Shop
541 US Route 1
☎ 207.869.5280

**Greenville**
Crazy Moose Fabrics
16 Pritham Avenue
☎ 207.696.3600

**Harmony**
Bartlett Yarns
20 Water Street
☎ 207.683.2251

**Hope**
Hope Spinnery
725 Camden Road
☎ 207.763.4600

**Kennebunk**
The Ball and Skein
169 Port Road #14
☎ 207.967.4434

**Lubec**
Wags & Wool
12 Water Street
☎ 207.733.4714

**New Sharon**
Imeldas Fabric & Design
5 Starks Road
☎ 207.778.0665

**Norway**
Fiber & Vine
402 Main Street
☎ 207.739.2664

**Portland**
KnitWit Yarn Shop
247A Congress Street
☎ 207.774.6444

Old Port Wool and Textile Company
52 Danforth Street
☎ 207.541.7429

Portland Fiber Gallery and Weaving Studio
50 Cove Street
☎ 207.780.1345

Tess' Designer Yarns
305 Commercial Street
☎ 207.460.9276

**Rockland**
Over The Rainbow Yarn
18 School Street
☎ 207.594.6060

Quilt Divas
607 Main Street
☎ 207.594.9447

**Scarborough**
Love to Knit Studio
27 Gorham Road
☎ 207.730.5598

**Skowhegan**
Happyknits
42 Court Street
☎ 207.474.7979

**South Portland**
Central Yarn Shop
868 Broadway
☎ 207.799.7789

**Southwest Harbor**
Quilt 'N' Fabric
11 Seal Cove Road
☎ 207.244.1233

**Standish**
Korner Knitters
2 Fort Hill Road
☎ 207.642.2894

Stockton Springs
Purple Fleece
103 School Street
☎ 207.323.1871

**Turner**
Nezinscot Farm
284 Turner Center Road
☎ 207.225.3231

**Waldoboro**
Eagles Nest Yarns
14 Old Route 1
☎ 207.832.6051

**Windham**
Rosemary's Gift & Yarn Shop
39 Roosevelt Trail
☎ 207.894.5770

**Woolwich**
Romney Ridge Farm
5 Meadow Road
☎ 207.442.7298

**York**
Yarn Sellar
264 Route U.S.1
☎ 207.351.1987

# Maryland

**Annapolis**
Yarn Garden
Festival at Riva Shopping Center
2303 Forest Drive
☎ 410.224.2033

**Baltimore**
Lovelyarns
3610 Falls Road
☎ 410.662.9276

That's the Point Needlecrafts
1005 S. Charles Street
☎ 410.347.7524

**Berlin**
A Little Bit Sheepish
2 S. Main Street
☎ 410.641.1080

**Bethesda**
Second Story Knits
4706 Bethesda Avenue
☎ 301.652.8688

**Boyds**
Knit Locally
15138 Barnesville Road
☎ 301.528.2800

**Catonsville**
Cloverhill Yarn Shop
77 Mellor Avenue
☎ 410.788.7262

**Chesapeake City**
Vulcan's Rest Fibers
106 George Street
☎ 410.885.2890

**Columbia**
All About Yarn
8970-G Route 108
☎ 410.992.5648

**Easton**
Blue Heron Yarns
8737 Brooks Drive
#108
☎ 410.819.0401

**Frivolous Fibers**
31 N. Harrison Street
☎ 410.822.6580

**Frederick**
The Knot House
129 East Patrick Street
☎ 334.707.0528

**Frostburg**
Frostburg Fiber Depot
9 W. Main Street
☎ 240.284.2154

**Glen Burnie**
The Knitting Boutique
910 Cromwell Park Drive
Suite 108
☎ 410.553.0433

**Glyndon**
Woolstock Knit & Sew
4830 Butler Road
☎ 410.517.1020

**Leonardtown**
Crazy for Ewe
22715 Washington Street
☎ 301.475.2744

**Ocean City**
Salty Yarns
807 Atlantic Avenue
☎ 410.289.4667

**Rockville**
Woolwinders
404 King Farm Boulevard
☎ 240.632.9276

**Sandy Spring**
So Original
900 Olney Sandy Spring Road
☎ 301.774.7970

**Silver Spring**
The Yarn Spot
11425 Grandview Avenue
☎ 301.933.9550

**Timonium**
Black Sheep Yarn Shop
9612 Deereco Road
☎ 410.628.9276

# Massachusetts

**Acton**
The Woolpack
340 Great Road
☎ 978.263.3131

**Adams**
A Stitch in Time
Rte 8 45 Commercial Street
☎ 413.743.7174

**Amherst**
The Creative Needle
233 N. Pleasant Street
☎ 413.549.6106

**Attleboro**
Yarn It All
1 Bank Street N.
☎ 508.695.3331

**Beverly**
Creative Yarns
16 Elliott Street
☎ 978.921.4673

Yarns in the Farms
641 Hale Street
☎ 978.927.2108

**Boston**
Bead + Fiber
460 Harrison Avenue
☎ 617.426.2323

Knit & Needlepoint
244 Newbury Street
☎ 617.536.9338

Newbury Yarns
166 Newbury Street
☎ 617.572.3733

Stitch House
846 Dorchester Avenue
☎ 617.265.8013

**Brookfield**
Knit Witts Yarn Shop
56 Allen Road
☎ 508.867.9449

**Burlington**
Edwina's Knitch
175 Cambridge Street
☎ 781.270.3617

**Cambridge**
Gather Here
370 Broadway
☎ 781.775.9405

Knittin' Kitten
93 Blanchard Road
☎ 617.491.4670

Mind's Eye Yarns
22 White Street
☎ 617.354.7253

**Charlton**
The Fabric Stash
45A Sturbridge Road
☎ 508.248.0600

**Dedham**
Sheep Skate Yarn and Craft
533 High Street
☎ 781.320.9276

**Deerfield**
Sheep & Shawl
265 Greenfield Road
☎ 413.397.3680

**Dennis**
Yarn Hound
620 Massachusetts 6A
☎ 508.385.6951

**Dudley**
Quilter's Loft
26 Mill Road
☎ 508.949.9095

**Duxbury**
Wool Basket Yarns
19 Depot Street
☎ 781.934.2700

**East Harwich**
Adventures in Knitting
105 Brewster Chatham Road/
Rte 137
☎ 508.432.3700

**Eastham**
The Yarn Basket
4205 State Highway
☎ 508.255.3557

**Easton**
Auntie Zaza's Fiber Works
104 Main Street
☎ 774.269.6899

**Essex**
Hooked Knitting
8 Martin Street
Suite 3
☎ 978.768.7329

**Fairhaven**
Eva's Yarn Shop
42 Main Street
☎ 508.996.5648

**Fall River**
KG Krafts
260 New Boston Road
☎ 508.676.3336

**Franklin**
Franklin Mill Store
305 Union Street
☎ 508.528.3301

**Gloucester**
Coveted Yarn
127 Eastern Avenue
Suite 4
☎ 978.282.8809

**Grafton**
Suzi's Fiber Cat
156 Main Street
☎ 508.839.3160

**Great Barrington**
Wonderful Things
232 Stockbridge Road
☎ 413.528.2473

**Groton**
Country Village Yarn Shop
6 W. Main Street
☎ 978.448.9276

**Harvard**
The Fiber Loft / Bare Hill
Studios
9 Mass Avenue
☎ 978.456.8669

**Hingham**
Yarns in the Square
28 South Street
☎ 781.749.2280

**Holden**
The Sheep Shack
787 Main Street
☎ 508.829.5811

**Ipswich**
Loom'n Shuttle
190 High Street Rt.1A
☎ 978.356.5551

**Jamaica Plain**
JP Knit and Stitch
461 Centre Street
☎ 617.942.2118

**Lenox**
Colorful Stitches
48 Main Street
(rear of bldg.)
☎ 800.413.6111

**Mashpee**
Yarn Basket
681 Falmouth Road
☎ 508.477.0858

**Melrose**
Sit 'N Knit
167 W. Emerson Street
☎ 781.662.9548

**Middleboro**
Spin-A-Bit
475 Plymouth Street
☎ 508.946.3343

**Nantucket**
Flock
14 Sparks Avenue
☎ 508.228.0038

**Natick**
Iron Horse
3 Pond Street
☎ 508.647.4722

**Needham**
Black Sheep Knitting Company
1500 Highland Avenue
☎ 781.444.0694

**Newburyport**
A Loom with a View
17 Green Street
☎ 978.463.9276

**Newton**
Knits & Pieces
8 Hale Street
☎ 617.969.8879

**North Billerica**
Hub Mills Store
16 Esquire Road, #2
☎ 978.408.2176

**North Falmouth**
Sage Yarn
660 North Falmouth Highway
☎ 508.457.9513

**Northborough**
Craftworks
243 W. Main Street
☎ 508.393.9435

**Northampton**
Northampton Wools
11 Pleasant Street
☎ 413.586.4331

WEBS - America's Yarn Store
75 Service Center Road
☎ 800.367.9327

**Orleans**
A Stitch in Thyme
2 Academy Place
☎ 508.247.9665

**Plainville**
In The Loop
60 Man Mar Drive
☎ 774.847.7977

**Plymouth**
Fancie Purls
170 Water Street
Unit 10
☎ 508.746.1746

**Rutland**
Knit 'n Stitch
10 Philips Road
☎ 508.886.6167

**Salem**
Seed Stitch Fine Yarn
21 Front Street
☎ 978.744.5557

**Sandwich**
Black Purls Yarn Shop
201 Route 6A
☎ 508.362.8880

**Shelburne Falls**
Metaphor Yarns
623 Mohawk Trail
☎ 413.625.9191

**Topsfield**
Village Stitchery
374 Boston Street
☎ 978.887.3083

**Uxbridge**
Yarn Shop
6 N. Main Street
☎ 508.278.7748

**Walpole**
Dee's Nimble Needles
15 West Street
☎ 508.668.8499

**Waltham**
The Island Yarn Company
85 River Street
☎ 781.894.1802

**West Boylston**
Knit One Quilt Two
244 W. Boylston Street
☎ 774.261.8393

**Weston**
In Stitches
454 Boston Post Road
☎ 781.891.4402

**Westport**
Sisters of the Wool
782 Main Road
☎ 774.264.9665

**Winchester**
Another Yarn
600 Main Street
☎ 781.570.2134

**Worcester**
Knitscape
1116 Pleasant Street
☎ 508.459.0557

# Michigan

**Ada**
Clever Ewe
596 Ada Drive SE
☎ 616.682.1545

**Alanson**
Dutch Oven Yarn Shop
7611 Burr Avenue
☎ 231.548.2700

**Allegan**
Marr Haven Wool Farm
772 39th Street
☎ 269.673.8800

**Alpena**
Spruce Shadow Farms Yarn Shop
2328 US 23, Alpena Mall
☎ 989.356.9434

Yarns to Go
127 North Second Avenue
☎ 989.356.4119

**Ann Arbor**
Busy Hands
306 S. Main Street #1C
☎ 734.996.8020

Ophir Crafts
2507 Jackson Avenue
Westgate Shopping Center
☎ 734.794.7777

**Bay City**
A Piece of Ewe
602 Saginaw Street
☎ 989.892.6400

The Stitching Well
78 State Park Drive
☎ 989.684.0231

Yarn Supply
3480 E. North Union Road
☎ 989.667.5308

**Beaverton**
Alli Mae's Fibernation
3354 M18
☎ 989.205.9697

**Beulah**
Yarn Market
244 S. Benzie Boulevard
Suite A
☎ 231.882.4640

**Berkeley**
Have You Any Wool?
3455 Robina Avenue
☎ 248.541.9665

**Birmingham**
The Knitting Room
251 East Merrill
☎ 248.540.3623

Right Off the Sheep
359 S. Old Woodward
☎ 248.646.7595

**Bridgman**
The Sandpiper
4217 Lake Street
☎ 269.465.5936

**Brighton**
Ewe-Nique Yarns
9912 E. Grand River Avenue
Suite 1300
☎ 810.229.5579

**Cadillac**
Knitter's Nest
10861 W. Cadillac Road
☎ 231.775.9276

**Caledonia**
Henny's Yarn Shop
131 E. Main Street
☎ 616.891.2406

**Caro**
Back Alley Fibers
142 N. State Street
☎ 989.672.2144

**Cedar**
Wool and Honey
9031 S. Kasson Street
☎ 231.228.2800

**Charlotte**
The Yarn Garden
111 W. Lawrence Avenue
☎ 517.541.9323

**Clare**
Apple Tree Lane
1606 N. McEwan
☎ 989.386.2552

**Clarkson**
Basketful of Yarn
5 South Main Street
☎ 248.620.2491

**Clawson**
PK Yarn over Knit
25 S. Main Street
☎ 248.808.6630

**Commerce Township**
Knitting on the Fringe
1717 Haggerty Road
☎ 248.624.7100

**Davison**
Elaine's Yarns
219 E. Flint
☎ 810.653.9010

**East Jordan**
Stonehedge Farm and Fiber Mill
2246 Pesek Road
☎ 231.536.2799

**Eaton Rapids**
Old Mill Yarn
109 E. Elizabeth Street
☎ 517.663.2711

**Elk Rapids**
Now & Then
126 River Street
☎ 231.264.5560

**Farmington**
Artisan Knitworks
23616 Farmington Road
☎ 248.427.0804

**Farmington Hills**
Fun with Fiber
33338 W. 12 Mile Road
☎ 248.553.4237

**Frankenmuth**
Rapunzel's Unique Gifts
and Yarns
664 South Main Street
☎ 989.652.0464

**Gladwin**
Yarn for Ewe
225 W. Cedar Avenue
☎ 989.709.5149

**Glen Arbor**
Plover Dunes
6640 W. Western Avenue
☎ 231.835.2067

The Yarn Shop
5917 S. Manitou Blvd. M-22
☎ 231.334.3805

**Grand Blanc**
Beyond the Rainforest Yarn Shop
12830 S. Saginaw Street
☎ 810.953.0089

**Grand Haven**
Needlesmith
109 N. 7th Street
☎ 616.844.7188

**Grand Rapids**
Field's Fabrics
3701 Plainfield Avenue NE
☎ 616.364.6505

A Grand Skein
2431 Eastern Avenue SE
☎ 616.551.1322

**Grayling**
Parrott's Perch Boutique
207 E. Michigan Avenue
☎ 989.348.2743

**Grosse Pointe**
The Wool and the Floss
397 Fisher Road
☎ 313.882.9110

**Grosse Pointe Woods**
Knotted Needle
20229 Mack Avenue
☎ 313.886.2828

**Harrison Township**
City Knits
26050 Crocker Boulevard
☎ 586.469.9665

**Hastings**
Jami's Craft Supplies
130 E. State Street
☎ 269.945.4484

Lady Peddler
142 E. State Street
☎ 269.948.9644

Walker Music & Textiles Co.
1450 W. State Street
☎ 269.804.6024

**Hessel**
Picklepoint
138 S. Pickford Avenue
☎ 906.484.3479

**Holland**
Friends of Wool
442 Washington Avenue
☎ 616.395.9665

**Houghton**
Sew Irresistible
407 Shelden Avenue
☎ 906.482.1722

**Howell**
Stitch in Time
722 E. Grand River Avenue
☎ 517.546.0769

**Hudsonville**
Painted Trillium Yarns
3500 Chicago Drive
☎ 616.669.4487

**Jackson**
Dropped Stitch
1212 Wildwood Avenue
Suite C
☎ 517.768.8280

**Jenison**
Country Needleworks
584 Chicago Drive
☎ 616.457.9410

**Kalamazoo**
Great Northern Weaving
451 E. D Avenue
☎ 269.341.9752

**Lake City**
Loney's Alpaca Junction
3109 N. 7 mile Road
☎ 231.229.4530

**Lake Linden**
Yarns & Threads
332 Calumet Street
☎ 906.296.9568

**Lansing East**
Old Town Sticks & Strings
1107 N. Washington Avenue
☎ 517.372.1000

Woven Art
325 Grove Street
☎ 517.203.4467

**Livonia**
Michigan Fine Yarns
37519 Ann Arbor Road
☎ 734.462.2800

**Ludington**
Nautical Yarn
108 S. Rath Avenue
☎ 231.845.9868

**Macomb**
Crafty Lady Trio
15401 Hall Road
☎ 568.566.8008

**Manistee**
Northern Spirits
389 River Street
☎ 231.398.0131

**Marquette**
Knitters Niche
1224 Division Street
☎ 906.228.9276

**Menominee**
The Elegant Ewe
400 First Street
☎ 906.863.2296

**Merrill**
Twisted Warp & Skeins
240 E. Saginaw Road
☎ 989.643.0108

**Milford**
The Knitting Circle
525 N. Main Street
☎ 248.684.1915

**Monroe**
Lake Erie Mercantile
15555 S. Telegraph Road
Suite 10
☎ 734.682.3945

**Newaygo**
The New Ewe Yarn
& Quilt Shoppe
59 W. State Road
☎ 231.652.5262

**Niles**
Red Purl
207 N. 2nd Street
☎ 269.684.0411

**Northport**
Dolls & More
104 Nagonaba Street
☎ 231.386.7303

**Ortonville**
Art of Life
391 Mill Street
☎ 248.627.4901

**Ottawa Lake**
Yarn Envy
4570 W. Sterns Road
☎ 734.856.1015

**Petoskey**
Cynthia's Too!
320 E. Mitchell Street
☎ 231.439.9221

**Plymouth**
Old Village Yarn Shop
42307 Ann Arbor Road E.
☎ 734.451.0580

**Portage**
Stitching Memories
350 Gladys Street
☎ 269.552.9276

**Richland**
Fabrications
8860 North 32nd Street
☎ 269.629.0190

**Richmond**
Sew Together
69295 Main Street
☎ 586.727.1555

**Rochester**
Skeins on Main
428 Main Street
☎ 248.656.9300

**Rockford**
JT Stitchery and Frame Shop
30 E. Bridge Street
☎ 616.866.2409

**Romeo**
Labor of Love Yarn
and Fiber Arts
246 N. Main Street
☎ 586.246.4724

Sheep Stuff/Michigan Farm
Woolies
6440 Boardman Road
☎ 313.798.2660

## Royal Oak
Ewe-Nique Knits
515 S. Lafayette
☎ 248.584.3001

## Saginaw
Grand Emporium Knitting Studio
5880 State Street
☎ 989.792.1234

The Little Yarn Shoppe
7075 Gratiot Rd Suite 4
☎ 989.274.8571

## South Haven
Needle in a Haystack
417 Phoenix Street
☎ 269.637.8216

## St. Charles
Victorian Purses by Sue
12640 S. Graham Road
☎ 989.865.6970

## St. Clair
Sweet PEA's Yarn & Gifts
201 N. Riverside Avenue
Riverview Plaza
☎ 810.329.2766

## St. Joseph
Ivelise's Yarn Shop
1601 Lake Shore Drive
☎ 269.925.0451

## Suttons Bay
Thistledown Shoppe
419 N. Joseph Street
☎ 231.271.9276

## Tawas East
Tawas Bay Yarn Co.
1820 East US 23
☎ 989.362.4463

## Traverse City
Lost Art Yarn Shoppe
741 Woodmere Avenue
☎ 231.941.1263

Yarn Quest
819 S. Garfield
☎ 231.929.4277

## Troy
My Craft Room
6020 Rochester Road
☎ 248.879.3360

## Vicksburg
Tanya's Girl Garage
123 S. Main Street
☎ 269.303.8817

## Whitmore Lake
Forma
111 E. Northfield Church Road
☎ 313.761.1102

## Williamston
Knitters' Nook
120 High Street
☎ 517.899.6759

## Wyoming
Threadbender Yarn Shop
2767 44th Street SW
☎ 616.531.6641

# Minnesota

**Anoka**
Shepherdess
2010 2nd Avenue N.
☎ 763.434.7453

**Battle Lake**
Prairie Needles
203 Lake Avenue S.
☎ 218.862.0094

**Bemidji**
Bemidji Woolen Mills
301 Irvine Avenue NW
☎ 218.751.5166

Yarn Dance
106 15th Street NE
☎ 218.333.6522

**Brainerd**
A 2 Z Yarn
1001 Kingwood Street
Suite 115
☎ 218.454.0133

Utrinkets
617 Laurel Street
☎ 218.454.9276

**Buffalo**
Silver Creek Cabin
3 Division Street W.
☎ 763.684.0554

**Burnsville**
Unwind Yarn Shop
14617 County Road 11
☎ 952.303.6617

**Cannon Falls**
What in Yarnation
402 Mill Street W.
☎ 507.263.0005

**Circle Pines**
Double Ewe Yarn Shop
9205 Lexington Avenue N., #3
☎ 763.795.9276

**Coon Rapids**
All about Yarn
455 99th Avenue NW
Suite 180
☎ 763.785.4900

Anoka Fiber Works
4153 Coon Rapids Blvd NW
☎ 763.479.9626

**Duluth**
Yarn Harbor
103 Mt Royal Shopping Circle
☎ 218.724.6432

**Ely**
Sisu Designs Knitting
31 W. Chapman Street
☎ 218.365.6613

**Excelsior**
Lakeside Yarn
347 Water Street
☎ 952.401.7501

**Grand Marais**
Raven's Beak Design
1823 W. Highway 61
☎ 218.387.2621

That Little Red House
113 West First Avenue
☎ 218.387.1094

**Grand Rapids**
Yarnworks
2036 S. Pokegama Avenue
☎ 218.326.9339

The Yarn Gallery
403 NW 1st Avenue
☎ 218.999.9922

**Hibbing**
Knitting Knight
113 East Howard Street
☎ 218.262.5764

**Knife River**
Playing With Yarn
276 Scenic Drive
☎ 218.727.5967

**Lindstrom**
Miss Elsie's Yarnery
12710 Lake Boulevard
☎ 651.257.6199

**Mahtomedi**
Lila and Claudine's Yarn and Gifts
86 Mahtomedi Avenue
☎ 651.429.9551

**Mankato**
Mary Lue's Yarn and Ewe
605 N. Riverfront Drive
☎ 507.388.9276

**Maple Grove**
Amazing Threads
11262 86th Avenue N.
☎ 763.391.7700

**Mendota Heights**
3 Kittens Needle Arts
750 Main Street
Suite 112
☎ 651.457.4969

**Minneapolis**
Crafty Planet
2833 Johnson Street NE
☎ 612.788.1180

Daisy Knits
819.49th Avenue NE
☎ 612.571.5744

Depth of Field Yarn
405 Cedar Avenue
☎ 612.340.0529

Digs Studio
3800 Grand Avenue S.
☎ 612.827.2500

Ingebretsen's
1601 East Lake Street
☎ 800.279.9333

Needlework Unlimited
4420 Drew Avenue S.
☎ 612.925.2454

StevenBe
3448 Chicago Avenue
☎ 612.259.7525

Textile Center
3000 University Avenue SE
☎ 612.436.0464

**Minnetonka**
Skeins
11345 Highway 7
☎ 952.939.4166

**New London**
Mitten Yarns at the Giving Tree
30 Main Street N.
☎ 320.354.4881

**New Ulm**
Nadelkunst
212 N. Minnesota Street
☎ 507.354.8708

**Northfield**
Northfield Yarn
314 Division Street
☎ 507.645.1330

**Park Rapids**
Monika's Quilt and Yarn Shop
210 Main Street
☎ 218.732.3896

**Princeton**
K & J Crafts
31351 Feldspar Street NW
☎ 763.389.1937

**Prior Lake**
Twisted Loop Yarn Shop
16210 Eagle Creek Avenue
☎ 952.240.8550

**Rochester**
Hank & Purl's Creative Nook
and Knittery
1623 N. Broadway
River Center Plaza
☎ 507.226.8045

Kelleys Quality Sewing Center
3432 55th Street NW
☎ 507.288.9051

**Rosemount**
The Yarn Garage
2980 145th Street W.
☎ 651.423.2253

**Sandstone**
Quarry Quilts & Yarns
326 Quarry Place
Suite 1
☎ 320.216.7639

**Street Cloud**
Bonnie's Spinning Wheel
16 21st Avenue S.
☎ 612.253.2426

Carole's Country Knits at
Rocking Horse Farm
25636 County Road 74
☎ 320.252.2996

Saint Louis Park
Linden Yarn & Textiles
5814 Excelsior Boulevard
☎ 952.303.3895

**St. Paul**
The Yarnery
840 Grand Avenue
☎ 651.222.5793

**Stillwater**
Darn Knit Anyway
423 Main Street S.
☎ 651.342.1386

**Superior**
Fabric Works
1320 Tower Avenue
☎ 715.392.7060

**Taylors Falls**
The Yarn Bank
406 Bench Street
☎ 651.465.6588

**Tofte**
Tall Tale Yarn Shop
7197 Bayview Drive
MN Highway 61
☎ 218.663.7557

**Waite Park**
Gruber's Quilt Shop
310 4th Avenue NE
☎ 320.259.4360

**White Bear Lake**
Sheepy Yarn Shoppe
2185 3rd Street
☎ 651.426.5463

**Winona**
Yarnology
65 East Third Street
☎ 507.474.9444

**Woodbury**
Knit'n from the Heart
1785 Radio Drive
☎ 651.702.0880

**Zumbrota**
BeeLighted Fiber & Gifts
386 Main Street
☎ 507.732.4191

Ellison Sheep Farm
15775 Highway MN -60
☎ 507.732.5281

# Mississippi

**Canton**
P is for Primitive
141 W. Peace Street
☎ 601.859.4252

**Diamondhead**
The French Knot
4406 Leisure Time Drive
☎ 228.255.3100

**Jackson**
The Knit Studio
1481 Canton Mart Road
Suite B
☎ 601.991.3092

**Oxford**
Knit1 Oxford
107 N. 13th Street
☎ 662.238.2829

**Petal**
The Yarn Basket
705 S. Main Street
☎ 601.582.7272

**Ridgeland**
The Southern Needle
500 Highway 51 N.
Suite T
☎ 601.919.7118

**Southaven**
Hank of Yarn
7075 Malco Boulevard
Suite 110
☎ 662.349.8883

**Starkville**
Fabriholics
108 MS 12
☎ 662.323.3899

**Yazoo City**
Knutty Knitters
(Inside Grace Hardware)
128 S. Main Street
☎ 662.746.7555

# Missouri

**Birch Tree**
The Twisted Thread Yarn Shop
501A East Old Highway 60
☎ 573.292.8002

**Branson**
Cecilia's Samplers
2652 Shepherd of the Hills Expressway
☎ 417.336.5016

**Columbia**
Carol Leigh's Hireek Fiber Studio
7001 Hireek Road
☎ 573.874.2233

Hireek Yarn Shoppe
601 Business Loop 70 W.
Suite 213C
☎ 573.449.5648

True Blew Yarns and More
1400 Forum Boulevard
Suite 10
☎ 573.443.8233

**Florissant**
Weaving Department at Myers House
180 W. Dunn Road
☎ 314.921.7800

**Forsyth**
The Yarn Diva
10726 MO-76
☎ 417.546.2037

**Independence**
Angelika's Yarn Store
500 N. Dodgion Street
☎ 816.461.5505

Knitcraft I
215 North Main Street
☎ 816.461.1248

**Jamesport**
Sue's Soft Stuff
205 S. Broadway
☎ 660.684.6205

**Mexico**
Treasure Chest Yarn Shop & More
216 W. Monroe
☎ 573.581.8007

**Kansas City**
Urban Arts and Crafts
4157 N. Mulberry Drive
☎ 816.234.1004

**Osage Beach**
The Yarn Basket
4681 US 54
☎ 866.915.1763

**Rogersville**
One City Market
214 Beatie Street
☎ 417.753.7100

**St. Charles**
Knit and Caboodle
423 S. Main Street
☎ 636.916.0060

**St. Joseph**
Red Barn Yarn Farm
1311 N. Belt Highway, Suite E.
☎ 816.752.5373

**St. Louis**
Hearthstone Knits
11429 Concord Village Avenue
☎ 314.849.9276

Kirkwood Knittery
10404 Manchester Road
☎ 314.822.7222

Knitorious
3268 Watson Avenue
☎ 314.646.8276

**Washington**
BAH! Yarns
805 Franklin
☎ 636.390.2400

**Webb City**
Stitch Space
111 N. Madison,
Suite #4
☎ 417.673.2240

**Weston**
Florilegium
367 Main Street
☎ 816.746.6164

# Montana

**Avon**
Birdseye Mercantile
105 Main Street W.
☎ 406.492.7070

**Big Timber**
Little Timber Quilts & Candy
108 McLeod Street
☎ 406.932.6078

**Bigfork**
Witty Knitters
8269 Mt. Highway 35
☎ 406.656.4999

**Billings**
Purl Yarn Boutique
1001 Shiloh Crossing Boulevard
Suite 2
☎ 406.652.4876

Wild Purls Yarns
1206 N. 24th Street W.
☎ 406.245.2224

**Bozeman**
Cnitting Bag
3 Cloninger Lane
☎ 406.587.2770

Stix
23 W. Main Street
☎ 406.556.5786

YarnScout
1203 N. Rouse
Suite 3C
☎ 406.577.2088

**Corvallis**
Mountain Colors Studio
1200 Eastside Highway
☎ 406.961.1900

**Dillon**
The Daily Yarn
36 N. Idaho Street
☎ 406.660.0597

**Dupuyer**
Beaverslide Dry Goods
307 Montana Street
☎ 406.472.3272

**Ennis**
Creations Yarn Shop
and Fiber Station
319 E. Main Street
☎ 406.682.3069

**Eureka**
The Woolery Mammoth
576 US Highway 93 N.
☎ 406.297.7403

**Fishtail**
Muddy Lamb Studio
25 W. Main Street
☎ 406.328.4788

**Fort Benton**
Stitch Away
1714 Front Street
☎ 406.622.4244

**Great Falls**
Pam's Knit 'N' Stitch
205 9th Avenue S.
Suite 102
☎ 406.761.4652

**Hamilton**
The Yarn Center
110 Pinckney Street
☎ 406.363.1400

**Helena**
Y'arnings
36 S. Last Chance Gulch
☎ 406.443.8073

**Kalispell**
Camas Creek Yarn
338 Main Street
☎ 406.755.9277

Woolen Collectibles
183 First Ave. E. N.
☎ 406.756.8746

**Livingston**
Back Porch Quilts
5237 US Highway 89 S.
Suite 14
☎ 406.222.0855

Thimbelina's Quilt Shop
118 N. B Street
Suite B
☎ 406.222.5904

**Missoula**
Beads, Yarns and Threads
2100 Stephens Avenue
☎ 406.543.9368

Joseph's Coat
115 S. 3rd Street W.
☎ 406.549.1419

**Polson**
All in Stitches
210 Main Street
☎ 406.883.3643

**Whitefish**
Knit 'n Needle
14 Lupfer Avenue
☎ 406.862.6390

**West Yellowstone**
Send It Home
30 Madison Avenue
☎ 406.646.7300

# Nebraska

**Hastings**
The Plum Nelly
743 W. 2nd Street
☎ 402.462.2490

**Lincoln**
Yarn Charm
4640 Bair Avenue
Suite 214
☎ 402.858.6300

The Yarn Shop
Sutter Place Mall
5221 S. 48th Street
☎ 402.489.9550

**Mitchell**
Brown Sheep Company
100662 County Road 16
☎ 308.635.2198

**Omaha**
For the Love of Stitching
2819 S. 125th Avenue
Suite 359, Westwood Plaza
☎ 402.884.1104

ImagiKnit
12100 W. Center Road
Suite 602
☎ 402.932.9525

Personal Threads Boutique
8600 Cass
☎ 402.391.7733

Wooly Mammoth Yarn Shop
2806 S. 110th Court
☎ 308.224.3824

**Stromsburg**
Spindle, Shuttle, and Needle
117 E. 4th Street
☎ 402.405.1971

# Nevada

**Carson City**
The Yarn Niche
512 N. Curry Street
☎ 775.841.1975

**Ely**
Creations
742 Aultman Street
☎ 775.289.7999

**Henderson**
Unwind Knitting
10545 S. Eastern Ave. #110
☎ 702.375.3070

**Las Vegas**
Sin City Knit Shop
2165 E. Windmill Lane
Suite 200
☎ 702.641.0210

**Minden**
Pioneer Yarn Company
1653 Lucerne Street
Suite B
☎ 775.392.3336

**Reno**
Jimmy Beans Wool
1312 Capital Boulevard #103
☎ 775.827.9276

**Stateline**
The Knitting Nest
472 Needle Peak Road
☎ 775.588.4015

# New Hampshire

**Amherst**
Covered Bridge Creations
141 Route 101-A M7
☎ 603.889.2179

**Antrim**
Artful Alpaca -Hidden Hill Farm
27 Mattheson Road
☎ 603.588.3370

The Wool Room at Meadow
Brook Farm
218 Pleasant Street
☎ 603.588.6637

**Center Harbor**
Patternworks Senter's Market
Route 25
☎ 603.253.9064

**Chester**
A Knitter's Garden
58 Derry Road
☎ 603.887.8550

**Claremont**
Frank's Bargain Center
Route 11/12 Charlestown Road
☎ 603.542.2218

**Concord**
The Elegant Ewe
75 South Main Street, #1
☎ 603.226.0066

**Deering**
Clark Summit Alpacas
Call for address
☎ 603.464.2910

**Derry**
The Yarn and Fiber Company
14 East Broadway
☎ 603.505.4432

**Durham**
Nordic Fiber Arts
Four Cutts Road
☎ 603.868.1196

**Exeter**
Charlotte's Web
137 Epping Road
☎ 603.778.1417

**Goffstown**
The Spotted Sheep
9 Church Street
☎ 603.660.1115

**Harrisville**
Harrisville Designs Retail Store
4 Mill Alley
☎ 603.827.3996

**Henniker**
The Fiber Studio
9 Foster Hill Road
☎ 603.428.7830

**Keene**
The Knitting Knook
36 Central Square
☎ 603.357.0516

New England Fabrics
55 Ralston Street
☎ 603.352.8683

**Lebanon**
Country Woolens
160 Mechanic Street
☎ 603.448.1840

**Littleton**
Yarn Garden
106 Main Street
☎ 603.444.5915

**Nashua**
Twill Fabric and Yarn
100 Main Street
☎ 603.718.1454

**Newport**
Hodgepodge Yarns & Fibers
45 Belknap Avenue
☎ 603.863.1470

**Plaistow**
Knit Pickings
18 Plaistow Road
☎ 603.382.5110

**Plymouth**
Inspire 2 Knit & Tea
12 Yeaton Road
☎ 603.536.5648

**Randolph**
Grand View Country Store
89 US Route 2
☎ 603.466.5715

**Wilton**
The Woolery
604 Gibbons Highway
Route 101
☎ 603.654.7030

**North Conway**
Close Knit Sisters
1976 White Mountain Highway
☎ 603.356.3777

# New Jersey

**Allentown**
The Quilter's Cottage
46 S. Main Street
☎ 609.259.5550

**Cape May**
Fiber Arts Yarn Shop
Washington Commons
315 Ocean Street, #23
☎ 609.898.8080

**Chatham**
The Stitching Bee
240a Main Street
☎ 973.635.6691

**Clark**
All about Ewe
5 Westfield Avenue
☎ 732.943.2763

**Collingswood**
Jubili Beads & Yarns
713 Haddon Avenue
☎ 856.858.7844

**Colts Neck**
Chelsea Yarns
340 State Route 34
☎ 732.637.8600

**Edison**
Knit Kit
1996 NJ-27
☎ 732.287.8177

**Englewood**
Expression Yarn Studio
13 E. Ivy Lane
☎ 201.569.4111

**Farmingdale**
A Stitch in Time
93 Main Street
Suite 100-A
☎ 732.938.3233

**Freehold**
Yarn Crafters
3333 Highway 9
☎ 732.308.0181

**Fort Lee**
Pat's Yarn Boutique
807 Abbott Boulevard
☎ 201.224.7771

**Frenchtown**
The Spinnery
33 Race Street
☎ 908.996.9004

**Haddonfield**
Hooked Fine Yarn Boutique
411 North Haddon Avenue
☎ 856.428.0110

**Hazlet**
Moore Yarn
1366 Route 36
Airport Plaza
☎ 732.847.3665

**Hillsborough**
Swallow Hill Farm
583 Montgomery Road
☎ 908.581.9912

The Yarn Attic
406 Route 206
☎ 908.864.5311

**Hillsdale**
Yarn Diva and More
428 Hillsdale Avenue
☎ 201.664.4100

**Hoboken**
Patricia's Yarns
107 Fourth Street
☎ 201.217.9276

**Jersey City**
2 Stix & A String
234 1/2 York Street
☎ 201.435.5408

**Lebanon**
Budding Star Quilts
1271 US Highway 22 E. #5
Lebanon Plaza
☎ 908.236.7676

**Madison**
Blue Purl
60 Main Street
☎ 973.377.5648

**Manalapan**
Knit1 Purl2
345 Route 9 S.
☎ 732.577.9276

**Maplewood**
Knitknack
1914 Springfield Avenue
☎ 973.327.2271

**Marlton**
Knitting Knook
25 E. Main Street
☎ 856.985.8042

**Metuchen**
The Brass Lantern
335 Main Street
☎ 732.548.5442

**Midland Park**
Close Knit
22 Paterson Avenue
☎ 201.891.3319

**Millville**
FiberArts Cafe
501 N. High Street
Suite L
☎ 856.669.1131

**Montclair**
Connie Sloan's Needle Craftique
594 Valley Road
☎ 973.783.7555

**Moorestown**
The Needleworks Barn
123 E. Main Street
☎ 856.235.7640

**Morristown**
Trillium Yarns
4 Cattano Avenue
☎ 973.425.0480

**Mt. Holly**
Woolbearers
90 High Street
☎ 609.914.0003

**Newton**
Yarn Boutique by Sarah
245 Spring Street
☎ 973.300.0255

**Ocean City**
The Knitting Niche
1330 Asbury Avenue
☎ 609.399.5111

**Pennington**
Knit One Stitch Too
16 N. Main Street
☎ 609.737.2211

**Pitman**
Karen's Needlecraft Shop
165 W. Jersey Avenue
☎ 856.589.4427

**Point Pleasant Beach**
Great Pacific Frame Shoppe
1004 Trenton Avenue
☎ 732.892.6207

**Princeton**
Pins and Needles
8 Chambers Street
☎ 609.921.9075

**Ridgefield Park**
Llama Llama Ewe
220 Main Street
☎ 201.931.6041

**Summit**
Wool & Grace
102 Summit Avenue
☎ 908.277.1431

**Teaneck**
Yarndevous
495 Cedar Lane
☎ 201.357.4710

**Verona**
I've got a Notion
269 Bloomfield Avenue
☎ 973.744.0079

**Vineland**
The Needleworks Barn
123 E. Main Street
☎ 856.235.7640

The Pin Cushion
657 N. Delsea Drive
☎ 856.692.5460

**Westfield**
Do Ewe Knit
217 Elmer Street
☎ 908.654.5648

Knit-A-Bit
66 Elm Street
Suite #2
☎ 908.301.0053

# New Mexico

**Albuquerque**
Fiber Chicks
206 1/2 San Felipe NW
Suite 9
☎ 505.242.6635

Fiesta Yarns Outlet Store
5620 Venice Avenue NE
Suite J
☎ 505.892.5008

Village Wools
5916 Anaheim Avenue NE
☎ 505.883.2919

The Yarn Store at Nob Hill
120 Amherst Drive
☎ 505.717.1535

**Corrales**
Lavender Lamb
3923 Corrales Road
☎ 505.792.7779

**Edgewood**
Edgewood Yarns and Fibers
95 State Road 344
Suite 2
☎ 505.286.8900

**Espanola**
Espanola Valley Fiber Arts Center
325 Paseo De Onate
☎ 505.747.3577

**Las Cruces**
Quillen Fiber Arts
121 Wyatt Drive #24
☎ 575.647.4050

**La Plata**
Skein Train
382 County Road 1191
☎ 505.325.2837

**Las Vegas**
ThreadBear
1813 Plaza Street
☎ 505.425.6263

**Los Ojos**
Tierra Wools
91 Main Street
☎ 575.588.7231

**Mora**
Mora Valley Spinning Mill
298 State Highway 518
☎ 575.387.2247

**Rio Rancho**
Enchanted Creations
1447 32nd Circle SE
☎ 505.892.8916

**Ruidoso**
The Stitching Post
1031 Mechem Drive
☎ 575.258.1732

**Santa Fe**
Looking Glass Yarn & Gifts
1807 2nd Street
Suite 2
☎ 505.995.9649

Miriam's Well
614 Paseo De Peralta
☎ 505.982.6312

Tutto Santa Fe
137 W. Water Street
☎ 505.989.9930

Yarn & Coffee
1836. B Cerrillos Road
☎ 505.780.5030

**Silver City**
Yada Yada Yarn
614 N. Bullard Street
☎ 575.388.3350

**Taos**
Mooncat Fiber
120B Bent Street
☎ 575.758.9341

**White Rock**
Warm Hearts
35 Rover Blvd
Suite D
☎ 505.672.2008

# New York

**Akron**
Daft Dames Handcrafts
13384 Main Road
☎ 716.542.4235

**Albany**
Trumpet Hill
Rosewood Plaza
501 New Karner Road
☎ 518.533.9622

**Alfred Station**
Alfred Knitting Studio
569 Main Street
☎ 607.587.8002

**Altamont**
The Spinning Room
190 Main Street
☎ 518.861.0038

**Amherst**
Have Ewe Any Wool
4551 Main Street
☎ 716.839.7800

**Arcade**
Creekside Fabrics, Quilts & Yarn
237 Main Street
☎ 585.492.4226

**Auburn**
All Tied Up Yarns
14 State Street
☎ 315.258.9276

**Babylon**
Village Knitter
57 West Main Street
Suite 130
☎ 631.321.7378

**Beacon**
Clay, Wood and Cotton
133 Main Street
☎ 845.481.0149

**Bemus Point**
Imagine!
4950 Main Street
☎ 716.386.2244

**Binghamton**
Spin A Yarn
9 Mitchell
☎ 607.722.3318

**Brocton**
Woolgathering
7 W. Main Street
☎ 716.467.3314

**Brooklyn**
Argyle Yarn Shop
288 Prospect Park W.
☎ 347.227.7799

B & E Yarn
784 Manhattan Avenue
☎ 718.383.8907

Brooklyn General Store
128 Union Street
☎ 718.237.7753

Fiber Notion
849 Union Street
☎ 718.230.4148

Knit-A-Way of Brooklyn
1970 Flatbush Avenue
☎ 718.797.3305

La Casita Yarn Shop
253 Smith Street
☎ 718.963.0369

Smiley's Yarns
92-06 Jamaica Avenue
Queens
☎ 718.849.9873

**Buffalo**
Elmwood Yarn Shop
1639 Hertel Avenue
☎ 716.834.7580

Have Ewe Any Wool
4551 Main Street
☎ 716.839.7800

Karma Knitting & Clothing
5546 Main Street
☎ 716.631.9276

**Burdett**
Graceful Arts Fiber Studio
4760 SR 414
☎ 607.546.8344

**Caledonia**
The Woolery on Main Street
3127 Main Street
☎ 585.538.9898

**Chatham**
The Warm Ewe
31 Main Street
☎ 518.392.2929

**Clinton**
The Two Ewes
4 Meadow Street
☎ 315.381.3024

**Cold Spring Harbor**
Loop on Main
143 Main Street
☎ 631.659.3810

**Colonie**
Lion Brand Yarn Shop
1814 Central Avenue
☎ 518.464.9276

**Cooperstown**
Line Drives & Lipstick
131 Main Street
Suite 1
☎ 607.437.1492

Sybil's Yarn Shop
1037 Route 166
☎ 607.286.7603

**Corning**
Wooly Minded
91 E. Market Street
☎ 607.973.2885

**Cornwall**
Cornwall Yarn Shop
227 Main Street
☎ 845.534.0383

**Cuddebackville**
Bonnies Kozy Knit
300 NY-211
☎ 845.754.0700

**Danby**
Susan's Spinning Bunny
311 Tupper Road W.
☎ 607.564.7178

**Delhi**
Yarn Shop
3428 Peakes Brook Road
☎ 607.746.3316

**East Aurora**
Knox Farm Fiber
Farm State Park
437 Buffalo Road
☎ 716.480.0086

The Woolly Lamb
712 Main Street
☎ 716.655.1911

**East Rochester**
The Village Yarn & Fiber Shop
350 W. Commercial Street
☎ 585.586.5470

**Elmira**
Malley's in the Yarn
767 South Kinyon Street
☎ 607.737.2765

**Endwell**
Cornucopia Yarns
2909 Watson Boulevard
☎ 607.748.3860

Yarns N' More
2605 East Main Street
☎ 607.786.9276

**Fairport**
Yarn Culture
1387 Fairport Road
Suite 885
☎ 585.678.4894

**Farmingdale**
Infinite Yarns
34B Hempstead Turnpike
☎ 516.293.0010

**Flushing**
Sandy's Knit 'n' Needles
154-03B Union Turnpike
☎ 718.380.0370

**Geneva**
The Yarn Shop of Geneva
508 Exchange Street
☎ 315.789.7211

**Genoa**
Fingerlakes Woolen Mill
1193 Stewarts' Corners Road
☎ 800.441.9665

**Ghent**
Turose
330B County Route 21C
☎ 518.672.0052

**Glendale**
Cook's Arts & Crafts Shoppe
80-09 Myrtle Avenue
Queens
☎ 718.366.6085

**Hamburg**
Embraceable Ewe Knitter's Retreat
213 Main Street
☎ 716.646.6674

**Hammondsport**
Fiber Arts Emporium
67 Shethar
☎ 607.569.3530

**Hartsdale**
Hartsdale Fabrics
275 S. Central Avenue
☎ 914.428.7780

**Hilton**
Amelia's Fabric & Yarn Shoppe
7 Upton Street
☎ 585.392.1192

**Hopewell Junction**
Out of the Loop
2593 Rte 52 Taconic Plaza
☎ 845.223.8355

**Hudson**
Countrywool
59 Spring Road
☎ 518.828.4554

Knit Wit Kreations
265 Main Street
☎ 518.747.4010

**Huntington**
The Knitting Corner
718 New York Avenue
☎ 631.421.2660

Knitting on the Lamb
50 Gerard Street
Suite 122
☎ 631.271.YARN

**Ithaca**
Homespun Boutique
314 E. State Street
☎     607.277.0954

Knitting, Etc.
2255 N. Triphammer Road
☎ 607.277.1164

**Jamesville**
Yarn Cupboard
6487 E. Seneca Turnpike
☎ 315.399.5148

**Kennedy**
Yarn for Ewe
Methodist Church
683 NY 394
☎ 716.267.2070

**Lake Placid**
Adirondack Yarns
2241 Saranac Avenue
☎ 518.523.9230

**Larchmont**
Etui Fiber Arts
2106 Boston Post Road
☎ 914.341.1426

Living Eden
29 West Market Street
☎ 845.475.2619

**Locke**
Grisamore Farms (seasonal)
749 Cowan Road
☎ 315.497.1347

**Manlius**
In-Stitches
206 E. Seneca Street
☎ 315.692.4090

**Marcellus**
Patchwork Plus Quilt and Yarn Shop
2532 Cherry Valley Turnpike
☎ 315.673.2208

**Marion**
Bead & Fiber Fantasy
4849 Cory Corners Road
☎ 315.926.5765

**Mattituck**
Altman's Needle & Fiber Arts
195 Love Lane
☎ 631.298.7181

**Mayville**
The Yarn Cottage
Located @ the Red Brick Farm
5031 W. Lake Road
☎ 716.753.5696

**Medina**
A Knitters Corner
111 West Center Street
☎ 585.798.5648

**Montgomery**
Montgomery Worsted Mills
23 Factory Street
☎ 845.457.9241

**Monticello**
Knit One Needlepoint Too
26 Thompson Square Mall
Route 42 N.
☎ 845.791.5648

**Nesconset**
Keep Me in Stitches
127-14 Smithtown Boulevard
☎ 631.724.8111

**New Paltz**
White Barn Farm Sheep
and Wool
815 Albany Post Road
☎ 914.456.6040

**New York City**
Annie & Company Needlepoint
and Knitting
1763 2nd Avenue
☎ 877.289.5648

Daytona Trimmings Company
Midtown West
251 W. 39th Street
☎ 212.354.1713

Downtown Yarns
45 Avenue A
☎ 212.995.5991

Gotta Knit
14 East 34th Street
☎ 212.989.3030

Habu Textiles
99 Madison Avenue
Suite 503
☎ 888.667.4030

Knitty City
208 W. 79th Street
☎ 212.787.5896

Lion Brand Yarn Studio
34 W. 15th Street
☎ 212.243.9070

Loop of the Loom
227 E. 87th Street
☎ 212.722.2686

Loopy Mango
78 Grand Street
☎ 212.343.7425

Purl Soho
459 Broome Street
☎ 212.420.8796

School Products Yarn
135 West 29th Street
Suite 402
☎ 212.679.3516

String
33 E. 65th Street
☎ 212.288.9276

Vardhman
269 W. 39th Street
☎ 212.840.6950

The Yarn Company
2274 Broadway
Suite 1C
☎ 212.787.7878

**North Syracuse**
Mission Rose Quiltery & Knittery
456 S. Main Street
☎ 315.452.3247

**Nyack**
Knitting Nation
30 North Broadway
☎ 845.348.0100

**Oceanside**
The Knitting Store
2 Poole Street
☎ 516.442.0722

**Oneonta**
Country Fabrics and Quilts and
April's Yarn Basket
5252 State Highway 23
☎ 607.432.9726

**Oxford**
Shadyside Fibers
109 Brown Road
☎ 607.843.8243

**Oyster Bay**
The Knitted Purl
80 South Street
☎ 516.558.7800

**Pattersonville**
A Touch of Twist
1286 Weast Road
☎ 518.864.5885

**Pawling**
Yarn & Craft Box
24 Charles Colman Boulevard
☎ 845.855.1632

**Pearl River**
The Stitchery
49 E. Central Avenue
☎ 845.735.4534

**Peekskill**
Cozy Corner Yarn Shop
116 Washington Street
☎ 914.737.0179

**Pittsford**
The Yarne Source
7 Schoen Place
☎ 585.662.5615

**Plainview**
Yarn Garden
661 Old Country Road
☎ 516.931.4909

**Plattsburgh**
Plattsburgh Yarn and Gifts
16 Brinkerhoff Street
☎ 518 593 3647

**Port Chester**
The Nimble Thimble
19 Putnam Avenue
☎ 914.934.2934

**Port Jefferson**
The Knitting Cove
207 E. Main Street
☎ 631.473.2121

**Port Washington**
The Knitting Place
191 Main Street
☎ 516.944.9276

**Potsdam**
Misty Hollow
22 Market Street
☎ 315.265.1660

**Queensbury**
The Yarn Angel
318 Ridge Street
☎ 518.761.2031

**Red Hook**
Hudson Valley Sheep and Wool
190 Yantz Road
☎ 845.758.3130

**Remsen**
Wool Haven Yarn & Fiber Shop
10071 Bardwell Mills Road
☎ 315.794.3769

**Rensselaer Falls**
Susan's Stitches
216B Rensselaer Street
☎ 315.344.5043

**Rhinebeck**
The Knitting Garage at Stickle's
13 E. Market Street
☎ 845.876.3206

**Rome**
Carol's Crafts
1245 Erie Blvd W.
☎ 315.336.3785

**Roslyn**
Knit
1353 Old Northern Boulevard
☎ 516.625.KNIT

**Saratoga Springs**
Common Thread
508 Broadway Street
☎ 518.583.2583

**Saugerties**
The Perfect Blend Yarn & Tea Shop
50 Market Street
☎ 845.246.2876

Pinewoods Farm Wool Shop
71 Phillips Road
☎ 845.246.2203

**Sayville**
Rumpelstiltskin Yarns
22 Main Street
☎ 631.750.1790

**Schuylerville**
The Yarn Shop at Foster Sheep Farm
460 West River Road
☎ 518.338.6679

**Staten Island**
The Naked Sheep
4038 Victory Boulevard
☎ 718.477.9276

**Sterling**
Maplegrove Wool Boutique
1275 State Route 104A
☎ 315.947.5408

**Syracuse**
Sheep Thrills
501 N. Main Street
☎ 315.458.0048

**Tarrytown**
Flying Fingers
15 Main Street
☎ 914.631.4113

**Tivoli**
Fabulous Yarn
60 Broadway
☎ 866.514.1127

**Troy**
Eastside Weavers
1 Carlyle Avenue
☎ 518.274.1931

**Valley Stream**
Knitting Store & More
232 Rockaway Avenue
☎ 516.561.7200

**Warsaw**
Dancing Goat Yarn Shop
11 West Buffalo Street
☎ 585.786.2888

**Watkins Glen**
FiberArts in the Glen
315 N. Franklin Street
☎ 607.535.9710

**Wayland**
Pollywogs Yarn & Fiber
7 Bush Avenue
☎ 585.728.5667

**Westfield**
Country Yarn Shoppe
6727 Sherman Westfield Road
☎ 716.326.2450

**Williamsville**
Karma Knitting
5546 Main Street
☎ 716.631.9276

**Woodhaven**
Smiley's Yarns
92-06 Jamaica Avenue
☎ 718.849.9873

# North Carolina

**Ahoskie**
Southern Purls
606 NC 561 E.
☎ 252.287.8469

**Apex**
DownTown Knits
122 N. Salem Street
☎ 919.249.5638

**Asheville**
Earth Guild
33 Haywood Street
☎ 828.255.7818

Friends & FiberWorks
800 Brevard Road
☎ 828.633.2500

The Knitting Diva
61 N. Merrimon Avenue
Suite 113
☎ 828.247.0344

Purl's Yarn Emporium
10 Wall Street
☎ 828.253.2750

**Black Mountain**
Black Mountain Yarn Shop
203 W. State Street
☎ 828.669.7570

**Blowing Rock**
Unwound
1132 Main Street
Suite 105
☎ 828.295.5051

**Burnsville**
YummiYarns
17 W. Main Street
☎ 828.678.9890

**Candler**
Friends and Fiberworks
19 Westridge Marketplace
☎ 828.633.2500

**Cary**
Shuttles, Needles, and Hooks
214 E. Chatham Street
☎ 919.469.9328

Warm 'n Fuzzy
200 S. Academy Street
Suite 140
☎ 919.380.0008

**Chapel Hill**
Yarns Etc.
99 S. Elliott Road
☎ 919.928.8810

**Charlotte**
Baskets of Yarn
1318 Central Avenue
Suite E3
☎ 704.733.9053

Charlotte Yarn
1235 East Boulevard
☎ 704.373.7442

The Fibre Studio at
Yarns to Dye For
4724 Sharon Road
Suite K
☎ 704.643.7720

Yarnhouse
2424 N. Davidson Street
☎ 704.335.8531

**Charlotte Mint Hill**
Cottage Yarn
7717 Matthews-Mint Hill Road
☎ 704.545.8440

**Davidson**
The Needlecraft Center
102 S. Main Street
☎ 704.892.8988

**Denver**
A Tangled Yarn Shop
3692 N. Highway 16
☎ 704.966.1300

**Durham**
Cozy
770 9th Street
☎ 919.286.3400

**East Murphy**
Yarn Circle
Peachtree Place
3851 Highway 64
Suite 6
☎ 828.835.4592

**Elizabeth City**
B&P Yarn Hut
1249 Highway 17 S.
Unit 3
☎ 252.333.3276

**Elkin**
Circle of Friends Yarn Shop
120 W. Main Street
☎ 336.526.3100

**Fayetteville**
All Things by Hand
25 Market Square
☎ 910.703.8585

Crafts Frames & Things
108 Owen Drive
☎ 910.485.4833

**Franklin**
Silver Threads & Golden Needles
41 E. Main Street
☎ 828.349.0515

**Gastonia**
Things Remembered Custom Framing
3805 S. New Hope Road
☎ 704.824.0473

**Greensboro**
Gate City Yarns
231 S. Elm Street
☎ 336.370.1233

Stitch Point
1614-C W. Friendly Avenue
☎ 336.272.2032

**Hatteras**
Blue Pelican Gallery Gifts and Yarn
57762 Highway 12
☎ 252.986.2244

**Henderson**
Yarny and Sassy
131 S. Garnett Street
☎ 252.432.5601

**Hendersonville**
Yarns to Dye For
927 Greenville Highway
☎ 828.697.0630

**Hickory**
Wildskeins Yarn Company
131 Highway 127 SE
☎ 828.322.9276

**High Point**
Common Threads Yarn Shop
1101 N. Main Street #201
☎ 336.889.8650

**Highlands**
Knit
310-D Main Street
☎ 828.482.1601

**Hillsborough**
Hillsborough Yarn Shop
114 S. Churton Street
☎ 919.732.2128

**Huntersville**
Knit One Stitch Too
9709 Sam Furr Road
☎ 704.655.9558

**King**
Papanana
145 Retail Circle
☎ 336.983.0400

**Kitty Hawk**
Knitting Addiction
3708 N. Croatan Highway, #2
☎ 252.255.KNIT

**Lenoir**
Chix with Stix
108 Main Street NW
☎ 828.758.0081

**Mars Hill**
Bovidae Farm
1186 Jarvis Branch Road
☎ 828.689.9931

Make It with Yarn
635 Carl Eller Road, #6
☎ 828.680.1500

**Mebane**
The Twisted Knitter
117 West Clay Street
☎ 919.563.2468

**Mint Hill**
Cottage Yarn
7717 Matthews Mint Hill Road
☎ 704.545.8440

**Morganton**
OSuzannah's Yarn on Union
130 W. Union Street
☎ 828.430.3300

**Mt. Airy**
What's Needlin' Ewe
411 N. Main Street
☎ 336.789.KNIT

**Murphy**
Yarn Circle
4400 E. U.S. Highway64 Alt
☎ 828.835.4592

**New Bern**
Weaver's Webb Gallery
602 Pollock Street
☎ 252.514.2681

**Pineville**
Rainy Day Creations
315 Main Street
☎ 704.889.1308

**Plymouth**
Yearning for Yarn
109 W. Water Street
☎ 919.482.2977

**Raleigh**
Great Yarns
1208 Ridge Road
☎ 919.832.3599

**Richlands**
The Tail Spinner
109 N. Wilmington Street
☎ 910.324.6166

**Saluda**
Kniticality
55 Robin Lane
☎ 828.749.3640

**Siler City**
Against His Will Gallery and Studio
117 E. Second Street
☎ 919.742.1122

Twin Birch Products
117 E. 2nd Street
☎ 919.742.1122

**Southern Pines**
Bella Filati Yarns
277 NE Broad Street
☎ 910.692.3528

**Southport**
Angelwing Needle Arts
507 N. Howe Street
☎ 877.454.9163

**Spencer**
TranqWool Knitting Provisions
516 S. Salisbury Avenue
☎ 704.431.4527

**Statesville**
Foothill Fiberarts
107 E. Broad Street
☎ 704.871.1030

**Swansboro**
Salty Sheep Yarn Shop
101-4 Church Street
☎ 910.325.0018

**Walnut Cove**
Thread Bear Quilt Shop
333 North Main Street
☎ 336.591.9221

**Wilmington**
The Quarter Stitch
5725 Oleander Drive
☎ 910.392.0020

Yarns of Wilmington
3401 Wrightsville Avenue
☎ 910.791.2157

**Winston Salem**
Knit One Smock Too
4003-A Country Club Road
☎ 336.765.9099

# North Dakota

**Beach**
Sip-in-Sew
22 Central Avenue
☎ 701.872.4226

**Bismarck**
Cedesigns & Yarn
417 E. Broadway Avenue
☎ 701.471.2131

**Bottineau**
Simple Threads Quilt Shop
120 11th Street W.
☎ 701.228.2180

**Dickinson**
Dakota Sew and So
2797 3rd Avenue W.
☎ 701.225.1408

**Fargo**
Prairie Yarns
2607 S. University Drive
☎ 701.280.1478

Bouclé Yarn Studio
616 Main Avenue
☎ 701.356.9276

**Garrison**
This That 'N More
62 N. Main Street
☎ 701.463.2671

**Minot**
The Yarn Stash
3305 4th Street SW #7
☎ 701.839.4099

**Valley City**
Quilted Ceiling
316 Central Avenue N.
Suite 101
☎ 701.845.4926

**Watford City**
Barrett Pharmacy
145 N. Main Street
☎ 701.842.3311

**Wishek**
J's Gift Shop
114 N. Centennial Street
☎ 701.452.2395

# Ohio

**Akron**
The Designing Woman
Merchant Square
137 Ghent Road
☎ 330.835.9400

**Albany**
Fiber FUN Studio
Gaston Road and Route 143
28743 Gaston Road
☎ 740.698.0101

**Ashland**
Suzie Homemaker
Fabrics-N-More
508 Claremount Avenue
☎ 419.752.9020

**Aurora**
The Knit Shop
226 S. Chillicothe Road
☎ 330.562.7226

**Bellefontaine**
The Sewing & Yarn Shop
118 N. Main Street
☎ 937.592.1885

**Berlin**
Helping Hands Quilt Shop
4818 State Route 39
E. Main Street
☎ 330.893.2233

**Bexley**
Betty's Yarn Shop
2451 Elm Avenue
☎ 614.231.7168

**Big Prairie**
Yarn and Bead Shop
9049 Trail 1043
☎ 330.496.3574

**Boardman**
Creekside Place Cafe & Shoppe
1449 Boardman-Canfield Road
☎ 330.726.4766

**Bowling Green**
The Busy Thimble
148 S. Main Street
☎ 419.806.4022

**Brecksville**
Crochet Innovations
7660 Chippewa Road
☎ 440.838.4455

**Canton**
The Artist's Gallery
1142 S. Main Street
☎ 330.494.8838

**Chagrin Falls**
Alpaca Fiber Studio & Friends
151 Bell Street
☎ 216.849.8850

The Artful Yarn
100 N. Main Street
Suite 230
☎ 440.321.9754

**Chardon**
Glacial Ridge Farm
10187 Thwing Road
☎ 440.477.6864

Knots -Knitting On the Square
153 Main Street
☎ 440.285.5648

**Chillicothe**
Unwind A Bit
14 W. Water Street
☎ 740.851.4407

**Cincinnati**
Fiber Licious
8157 Camargo Road
☎ 513.271.3191

Fiberge
1407 Vine Street
☎ 513.831.9276

Hank, a Yarn Boutique
2651 Observatory Avenue
☎ 513.386.9869

One More Stitch
1609 Madison Road
☎ 513.533.1170

Silk Road Textiles
6106 Hamilton Avenue
☎ 513.541.3700

**Cleveland**
Fine Points
12620 Larchmere Boulevard
☎ 216.229.6644

**Cleveland Heights**
Susan Yarns
2132 South Taylor Road
☎ 216.321.2687

**Clyde**
The Little House
1927 N. Main Street
☎ 800.554.7973

**Columbus**
Knitters Mercantile
214 Graceland Blvd
☎ 614.457.7836

The Yarn Shop
1125 Kenny Centre Mall
☎ 614.888.8551

**Coshocton**
Mercantile on Main
603 Main Street
☎ 740.622.5956

**Creston**
Moonstruck
9874 Cleveland Road
☎ 330.435.6669

**Dayton**
Busy Beaver Arts & Crafts
3445 Dayton Xenia Road
☎ 937.429.3920

Fiberworks
1350A N. Fairfield Road
Beavercreek
☎ 937.429.9276

New World Alpaca Textiles
PNC 2nd Street Market
600 E. 2nd Street
☎ 937.287.2284

Strings Attached
225 N. Main Street
☎ 937.221.9585

**Defiance**
The Fifth Stitch
300 Clinton Street
☎ 419.782.0991

**Dublin**
Knitting Temptations
35 S. High Street
☎ 614.734.0618

What's the Point?
126 S. High Street
☎ 614.717.9008

**Findlay**
Craft Gallery
406 Walnut Street
☎ 419.422.7980

Yarn Farm
11610 Township Road 180
☎ 419.423.4252

**Grafton**
That'll Do Farm
34634 Ohio 303
☎ 440.829.3644

**Grand Rapids**
Natural Fiber and Yarn Company
24122 Front Street
☎ 419.832.5648

**Green Uniontown**
My Sister's Yarn Shop
3477 Massillon Road
☎ 330.896.7040

**Hamilton**
Lambikin's Hideaway
Yarn & Stitchery
217 S. B Street
☎ 513.895.5648

**Hillsboro**
Margaret's Memories
220 W. Beech Street
☎ 937.763.1831

**Lakeside**
Christi's Just For Ewe Yarn Shop
9523 E. Harbor Road
☎ 419.798.5499

**Lakewood**
River Colors Studio
1387 Sloane Avenue
☎ 216.228.9276

**Lima**
Heavenly Stitches
2696 Greely Chapel Road
☎ 419.905.5950

**Lodi**
Black Locust Farm
110 Bank Street
☎ 330.948.9276

**Maderia**
Fiberlicious
8157 Camargo Road
☎ 513.271.3191

**Mansfield**
Alpaca Meadows
1200 Rock Road
☎ 419.529.8152

**Marblehead**
Just for Ewe
9523 E. Harbor Road
Route 163
☎ 888.798.4ewe

**Marietta**
Quilter's Corner
400 Tennis Center Drive
☎ 740.373.6150

**Marion**
Spin a Yarn Fiber Garden
187 W. Center Street
☎ 740.382.6969

**Marysville**
Lonestar Quilting
1055 W. Fifth Street
☎ 937.644.1234

**Mason**
Main Street Yarns
126 W. Main Street
☎ 513.204.0078

**Medina**
Studio Knit
28 Public Square
☎ 330.241.5608

**Miamisburg**
The Little Shop of Stitches
79 S. Main Street
☎ 937.384.0804

**Middlefield**
The Craft Cupboard
14275 Old State Road
☎ 440.632.5787

**Milton**
Wertz's Variety
6 N. Main Street W.
☎ 937.698.5212

**Minster**
The Thankful Ewe/
Paper and Yarn
56 W. 4th Street in downtown
☎ 419.628.1300

**New Albany**
The Knitting Nomad
4101 Audley Road
☎ 614.939.9935

**Newark**
Lola's Alpaca Shop
2653 Swans Road NE
☎ 740.345.2199

**New Waterford**
Embroidered 4 You & Yarn 2
5577 State Route 7
☎ 330.457.0351

## Oberlin
Ginko Gallery & Studio
19 S. Main Street
☎ 440.774.3117

Smith Furnishings
25 W. College Street
☎ 440.774.2371

## Pepper Pike
Ewes d' Bleu Yarns of Distinction
30559 Pinetree Road
Suite 206
☎ 216.644.4550

## Perrysburg
Yarn Cravin'
146 E. 2nd Street
☎ 419.872.9276

## Pickerington
Yarnmarket
12936 Stonecreek Drive
☎ 888.996.9276

## Richfield
Cornerstone Yarns
Richfield Commons
4174 Wheatley Road
☎ 330.659.2669

## Salem
Knit-Wit Knits
645 East State Street
☎ 330.337.5648

## Sardinia
Ohio Valley Natural Fibers
8541 Louderback Road
☎ 937.446.3045

## Sebring
Heidi and Lana
222 North 15th Street
☎ 330.257.9292

## Shreve
Noah's Landing
7276 Aylsworth Road
☎ 330.496.9065

## South Bloomfield
VonStrohm Fiber
Processing Mill
5010 N. Walnut Street
☎ 740.983.2042

## Springboro
Wooly Bully Yarn Company
135 S. Main Street
☎ 937.748.1002

## Tipp City
Tippecanoe Weaver
and Fibers Too
17 N. Second Street
☎ 937.667.5358

## Toledo
Yarn Company
4434 Secor Road
☎ 419.474.6744

## Wadsworth
Sally's Shop
141 College Street
☎ 330.334.1996

**Zanesville**
The Alpacas of Spring Acres
Farm Store
3390 Big B Road
☎ 740.796.2195

# Oklahoma

**Allen**
Prairie Notions
701 E. Gilmore Street
☎ 580.857.2831

**Antlers**
Betsy's Quilts and Fabric Shop
419580 E. 1930 Road
☎ 580.298.5821

**Bartlesville**
Carrico's Creative Corner
(By appt. only)
20873 N. 4040 Road
☎ 918.333.8933

**Claremore**
Unwind a Yarn Shop
632 E. Will Rogers Boulevard
☎ 918.342.9276

**Durant**
HNT Quilt Shop
137 W. Main Street
☎ 580.924.7837

**Grove**
Ewe and Me
916 South Broadway Street
☎ 918.786.3588

**Guthrie**
Sealed With A Kiss
109 E. Oklahoma
☎ 405.282.8649

**Mangum**
The Busy Bee
120 E. Lincoln Street
☎ 580.782.3805

**Norman**
L & B Yarn Co.
425 W. Gray Street
☎ 405.310.3636

**Oberlin**
Criation Station Alpaca Farm
13790 Quarry Road
☎ 440.774.2451

**Oklahoma City**
The Gourmet Yarn Co.
9638 N. May Avenue
☎ 405.286.3737

**Pauls Valley**
Gallery
204 W. Paul Avenue
☎ 405.207.9527

**Perkins**
Main Street Mall Hook Nook
111 South Main Street
☎ 405.547.2044

**Tulsa**
Get Stitchin'
6011 S. Sheridan Road
☎ 918.481.1055

Stitches of Tulsa
5944 S. Lewis Avenue
☎ 918.747.8838

**Watonga**
Loops
6034 S. Yale Avenue
☎ 918.806.6100

Sweetie Wray's ...A Yarn Shop
113 W. Main Street
☎ 580.623.2112

# Oregon

**Ashland**
The Websters
11 N. Main Street
☎ 541.482.9801

**Astoria**
Astoria Fiber Arts Academy
1292 Duane Street
☎ 503.325.9285

Custom Threads
1282 Commercial
☎ 503.325.7780

**Aurora**
Beyond Art
21497 Pacific Highway E.
☎ 503.678.2633

**Bandon**
Stranded by the Sea
390 1st Street SW
☎ 541.329.0185

The Wool Company
990 2nd Street SE
☎ 541.347.3912

**Beaverton**
For Yarn's Sake
11679 SW Beaverton-Hillsdale Highway
☎ 503.469.9500

Nitro Knitters
10047 SW Nimbus Avenue
☎ 503.372.9318

**Bend**
All Ways Wild & Wooly
22390 McArdle Road
☎ 541.280.6609

Gossamer: The Knitting Place
1326 NW Galveston Avenue
☎ 541.383.2204

**Brookings**
By My Hand
1109 Chetco Avenue
☎ 541.412.0917

**Brownsville**
Brownsville Stitching Parlor
113 Spaulding Way
☎ 541.466.3660

**Canby**
Fantasy Fibers
9190 S. Centennial Lane
☎ 503.263.4902

**Cannon Beach**
Coastal Yarns
255 N. Hemlock A1
☎ 503.436.1128

**Coos Bay**
My Yarn Shop
264 Broadway
☎ 541.266.8230

**Corvallis**
Creative Crafts & Frame Shop
934 NW Kings Boulevard
☎ 541.753.7316

Stash
110 SW 3rd Street
☎ 541.753.9276

**Cresswell**
Mountain Shadow Ranch
83208 Rodgers Road
☎ 541.895.5512

**Eugene**
Beacon Bend Alpacas
865 E. Beacon Drive
☎ 541.302.9455

Eugene Textile Center
1510 Jacobs Drive
☎ 541.688.1565

The Knit Shop
2811 Oak Street
☎ 541.434.0430

Soft Horizons Fibre
412 East 13th Avenue
☎ 541.343.0651

Textiles a Mano
965 Tyinn Street
☎ 541.485.6266

**Florence**
Happy Kampers Yarn Barn
88878 Highway 101
☎ 541.997.9414

**Forest Grove**
Spin a Good Yarn
1703 Pacific Avenue
☎ 503.648.8525

**Gilchrist**
Dragonfly Yarn & Gifts,
138312 Michigan Avenue
☎ 541.771.2248

**Gleneden beach**
In the Wind Yarns
7755 Highway U.S.101
☎ 541.764.3333

**Gold Beach**
By My Hand
29795 Ellensburg Avenue
☎ 541.247.0133

**Grants Pass**
Bead Merchant and Yarn Supply
300 SE 6th Street
☎ 541.471.0645

**Hermiston**
The Material Girl Quilt Shop
1565 N. 1st Street, Suite 7
☎ 541.289.2555

## Hillsboro
Black Sheep at Orenco
6154 NE Brighton Street
☎ 971.732.5391

## Hood River
Foothills Yarn & Fiber
4207 Sylvester Drive
☎ 541.354.3542

Knot another Hat
16 Oak Street #202
☎ 541.308.0002

## John Day
Skeins
516 S. Canyon Boulevard
☎ 541.575.5648

## Klamath Falls
Laize~Dayz Yarn & Tea Shoppe
2617 Pershing Way
☎ 541.887.8560

## Langlois
Wild Rivers Wool Factory
48443 Highway 101
☎ 541.348.2033

## Lebanon
Knitty Gritty Yarn Store
285 South Main Street
☎ 541.936.4677

## Manzanita
T-SPOT Yarn, Teas and Chocolates
144 Laneda Avenue
☎ 503.368.SPOT

## McMinnville
Oregon Knitting Co.
309 Northeast Baker Street
☎ 971.261.9608

## Milton-Freewater
Oregon Trail Yarn
1112 S. Main
☎ 541.938.4451

## Milwaukie
Mill End Store
9701 SE McLoughlin Boulevard
☎ 503.786.1234

## Medford
Jenny's Yarn Shop
30 N. Central
☎ 541.734.8800

## Newberg
Pacific Wool and Fiber
2505 Portland Road
Suite 104
☎ 503.538.4741

## Newport
Yarn For All Seasons
3101 SE Ferry Slip Road
#232
☎ 541.867.3411

## Oregon City
Knit-A-Bit
16925 South Beckman Road
☎ 503.631.4596

## Portland
Close Knit
2140 NE Alberta Street
☎ 503.288.4568

Dublin Bay Knitting Company
1227 NW 11th Avenue
☎ 503.223.3229

Fabric Depot
700 SE 122nd Avenue
☎ 503.252.9530

Gossamer
2418 E. Burnside Street
☎ 503.233.4807

Happy Knits
1620 SE Hawthorne Boulevard
☎ 503.238.2106

Knit/Purl
1101 SW Alder Street
☎ 503.227.2999

Knitting Bee
10934 SW Barnes Road
☎ 503.439.3316

Knittn' Kitten
7530 NE Glisan Street
☎ 503.255.3022

The Naked Sheep Knit Shop
2142 N. Killingsworth Street
☎ 503.283.2004

Northwest Wools
3524 SW Troy
☎ 503.244 .5024

Pearl Fiber Arts
428 NW 11th Avenue
☎ 503.227.7746

Pendleton Woolen Mill Store
8500 SE McLoughlin Boulevard
☎ 503.535.5786

Twisted
2310 NE Broadway Street
☎ 503.922.1150

Yarn Garden
1413 SE Hawthorne Boulevard
☎ 503.239.7950

Yarnia
3773 SE Belmont
☎ 503.939.5338

**Roseburg**
Knotty Lady Yarns
642 SE Jackson
☎ 541.673.2199

Jackson St Fiber Arts
556 SE Jackson Street
☎ 541.672.9276

**Sandy**
Designer Yarn
38871 Proctor Boulevard
☎ 503.826.0123

**Salem**
Tangled Purls
2290 Commercial Street SE
Suite 140
☎ 503.339.7556

Teaselwick Wools
1313 Mill Street SE
☎ 503.586.0232

**Seaside**
Creative Beginnings
620 S. Holladay Drive
Suite 1
☎ 503.738.9580

**Silverton**
Apples to Oranges
206 Oak Street
☎ 503.874.4901

**Sisters**
Desert Charm
161 S. Elm Street
☎ 541.549.8479

The Stitchin' Post
311 W. Cascade
☎ 541.549.6061

**St. Helens**
Mo's Art, Hook & Needle
161 Street Helens Street
☎ 503.366.9276

The Dalles
The Whole Ball of Yarn
413 E. 2nd Street
☎ 541.506.9276

**Tigard**
All about Yarn
11945 SW Pacific Highway
☎ 503.684.4851

**Tillamook**
Jane's Fabric Patch
1110 Main Avenue
☎ 503.842.9392

Latimer Quilt & Textile Center
2105 Wilson River Loop
☎ 503.842.8622

Tangled Yarns
207 Main Avenue
☎ 541.418.2329

**Union**
Knitkabob
156 South Main
☎ 541.562.2276

**West Linn**
Wool N' Wares Yarn Shop
21540 Willamette Drive
☎ 503.657.7470

# Pennsylvania

**Allentown**
Tucker Yarn Shop
950 Hamilton Street
☎ 610.434.1846

**Altoona**
Moore Stitches
1635 E. Pleasant Valley Boulevard
☎ 814.943.2977

**Bedford**
Firesong Studio
201 W. Penn Street
☎ 814.623.0776

**Berwyn**
Froufrou
601 Lancaster Avenue
☎ 610.296.8597

**Bethlehem**
The Knitter's Edge
1601 W. Broad Street
☎ 610.419.9276

**Bird In Hand**
Labadie Looms
2572 Old Philadelphia Pike
☎ 717.291.8911

**Bridgeville**
Kid Ewe Knot
429 Washington Avenue
Suite 4
☎ 412.257.2557

**Brookville**
Spin-A-Yarn
360 Main Street
☎ 814.849.2512

**Chadds Ford**
A Garden of Yarn
34 Old Ridge Village
☎ 610.459.5599

**Chambersburg**
Yarn Basket
150 Falling Spring Road
☎ 717.263.3236

**Chestnut Hill**
The Knit with Yarn Shop
8226 Germantown Avenue
☎ 215.247.YARN

**Clarks Summit**
Summit Yarn Studio
276 E. Grove Street
☎ 570.383.4994

**Coudersport**
Yarn at Olga's
107 E. 2nd Street
☎ 814.274.0794

**Covode**
Autumn House Farm
1001 Locust Road
☎ 724.286.9596

**Danville**
Swisher's Yarn Basket
327 Ferry Street
☎ 570.275.9276

**Doylestown**
Forever Yarn
15 W. Oakland Avenue
☎ 215.348.5648

**DuBois**
The Ewe-nique Sheep
200 Commons Drive
☎ 814.372.2230

**East Berlin**
The Mannings Handweaving School
1132 Green Ridge Road
☎ 717.624.2223

**East Stroudsburg**
Mountain Knits & Pearls
114 Washington Street
Suite 100
☎ 570.424.7770

**Emmaus**
Conversational Threads Fiber
Arts Studio
6 S. 4th Street on the Triangle
☎ 610.421.8889

**Erie**
Cultured Purl
3141 W. 26th Street
☎ 814.836.7875

Rustic & Refined
2598 W. 8th Street
☎ 814.838.1710

**Everett**
Eweknit
22 N. Spring Street
☎ 814.348.1020

**Franklin**
Diane's Gift Boutique
1261 Elk Street
☎ 814.671.0401

**Glenside**
Stitchers' Dream
221 S. Easton Road
☎ 215.885.3780

**Grove City**
Wolf Creek Yarns
112 Blair Street
☎ 724.458.5290

**Hamburg**
Yarns R Us
700 S. 4th Street
☎ 610.562.5629

**Harmony**
Darn Yarn Needles and Thread
253D Mercer Street
☎ 724.473.0983

**Harrisburg**
Knitters Dream
605 LeSentier Lane
☎ 717.599.7665

**Havertown**
Stash
2120 Darby Road
☎ 484.416.3649

**Hollidaysburg**
Delightful Ewe
200 Bedford Street
☎ 814.696.033

**Honesdale**
The Gentle Arts
1043 Main Street
☎ 570.352.3352

**Indiana**
Yarns
1136 Philadelphia Street
☎ 724.349.3240

**Intercourse**
Lancaster Yarn Shop
3519 Old Philadelphia Pike
Kitchen Kettle Village
☎ 717.768.8007

**Kingston**
Gosh Yarn It!
303 Market Street
☎ 570.287.9999

**Lahaska**
Twist Knitting and Spinning
5743 Route 202
☎ 215.794.3020

**Lancaster**
Oh Susanna
2204 Marietta Avenue
☎ 717.393.5146

The Speckled Sheep
713 Olde Hickory Road
☎ 717.435.8359

**Landisville**
Flying Fibers
329 Main Street
☎ 717.898.8020

**Lansdale**
The Lamb's Wool
32 East Blaine Street
☎ 215.361.9899

**Lebanon**
Martin's Fabrics & Craft Barn
2799 E. Cumberland Street
☎ 717.274.5359

**Ligonier**
Bo-Peep Fine Yarns
221 West Main Street
☎ 724.238.4040

Kathy's Kreations
141 East Main Street
☎ 724.238.9320

**Lititz**
The Ball and Skein Shop
2 E. 28th Division Highway
Route 322
☎ 717.625.4280

**Mansfield**
Yorkshire Meadows
North Elk Run Road
☎ 570.549.2553

**Muncy**
Glenda's Knit Knook
2729 Lycoming Mall Drive
☎ 570.546.9550

**Nazareth**
Kraemer Yarn Shop
240 S. Main Street
☎ 610.759.1294

**New Hope**
Gazebo Plus
7 Village Row
☎ 215.862.0740

**Newtown Square**
Slip Knot
3719 W. Chester Pike
☎ 610.359.9070

**Oakdale**
Tonidale Yarn & Needlecraft
1050 Montour Church Road
☎ 412.788.8850

**Oakmont**
Yarns by Design
622 Allegheny River Boulevard
☎ 412.794.8332

**Perkasie**
Lillie's Yarns
1000 E. Walnut Street
Suite 204
☎ 215.258.1259

**Pittsburgh**
Dyed in the Wool
3458 Babcock Boulevard
☎ 412.364.0310

Knit One
2721 Murray Avenue
☎ 412.421.6666

**Natural Stitches**
The Village of East Side
6401 Penn Avenue
☎ 412.441.4410

**Philadelphia**
Hidden River Yarns
4358-B Main Street
☎ 215.920.2603

The Knit With
8226 Germantown Avenue
☎ 215.247.YARN

Loop
1914 South Street
☎ 215.893.9939

Nangellini
1030 N. 2nd Street #301
☎ 215.413.5001

Rosie's Yarn Cellar
2017 Locust Street
☎ 215.977.9276

Yarnphoria
1016 Pine Street
☎ 215.923.0914

**Quakertown**
Juniper Place Yarns
132 E. Broad Street
☎ 215.536.4449

**Rochester Mills**
Autumn House Farm & Heritage Artworks
1001 Locust Road
☎ 724.286.9596

Ewe Can Knit
417 Wood Street
☎ 412.281.0123

The Tangled Web
7709 Germantown Avenue
☎ 215.242.1271

**Pike Penns Park**
Knitting to Know Ewe
2324 Second Street
☎ 215.598.9276

**Scranton**
The Gentle Arts
1425 Ash Street
☎ 570.955.0317

**Sewickley**
Yarns Unlimited
435 Beaver Street
☎ 412.741.8894

**Shiremanstown**
Colonial Yarn Shop
7 Front Street
☎ 717.763.8016

**Skippack**
Yarnings
4007 Skippack Pike
☎ 610.584.6216

**Spring Mills**
The Knitter's Underground
532 Lower Georges Valley Road
☎ 800.693.7242

**Swarthmore**
Finely a Knitting Party
104 Park Avenue
☎ 610.328.7210

**Warren**
Dreamboat Hobbies
21690 Route 6
☎ 814.723.8052

**Watsontown**
Glory-ous Knits and Gifts
15 Harris Circle
☎ 570.437.4139

**Waynesboro**
The Knitting Cottage
6810 Iron Bridges Road
☎ 717.762.1168

**West Reading**
The Yarn Gallery
628 Penn Avenue
☎ 610.373.1622

**Willow Street**
Legacy Yarn Company
2611 Willow Street Pike
☎ 717.464.7575

**Yardley**
Y Knot Knit
79 South Main Street
☎ 215.321.2170

**York**
Uncommon Threads
2081 Springwood Road
☎ 866.323.9276

# Rhode Island

**Block Island**
North Lights Fibers
129 Spring Street
☎ 401.466.2050

**Central Falls**
Peter Patchis Yarns
174 Cross Street
☎ 401.723.3116

**Chepachet**
Sue's Yarn Basket
29 Dorr Drive
☎ 401.567.0540

**East Greenwich**
Love2Knit
5600 Post Road
Suite 124
☎ 401.398.7939

**Exeter**
Eneri Knits
567 S. County Trail
Suite 106
☎ 401.294.1255

**Greenville**
Wood Items & More
576 Putnam Pike
☎ 401.949.3550

**Middletown**
Knitting Corner and Beadery
575 E. Main Road
☎ 401.619.2120

**Newport**
Knitting Needles
555 Thames Street
☎ 401.841.5648

**North Kingstown**
The Mermaid's Purl
1 W. Main Street
☎ 401.268.3899

**Pawtucket**
Wayland Yarn Shoppe
112 Raleigh Avenue
☎ 401.726.4696

The Yarn Outlet
50 Division Street
☎ 401.722.5660

**Tiverton**
Perfectly Twisted Yarn
651 Main Road
☎ 401.816.0043

Sakonnet Purls
3988 Main Road
☎ 401.624.9902

**Wakefield**
Two Dots
344 Main Street
☎ 401.783.2045

**Warren**
Bella Yarns
476 Main Street
☎ 401.247.7243

**Woonsocket**
Yarnia
285 Main Street
☎ 401.762.0671

# South Carolina

**Aiken**
NeedleWorks
345 Hayne Avenue
☎ 803.644.0990

**Beaufort**
Coastal Knitting
900 Port Republic Street
☎ 843.470.0148

**Easley**
The Knitting & Lacemaking Cottage
438 Crossroads Church Road
☎ 864.850.0103

**Georgetown**
Prena Knits
800 Front Street
☎ 843.545.5344

**Greenville**
The Needle Tree
22 Tindal Avenue
☎ 864.235.6060

Yarn & Yall
600 Laurens Road
☎ 864.239.2222

**Hilton Head Island**
The Courtyard
32 Palmetto Bay Road
#10A
☎ 843.842.5614

**Johns Island**
It's A Stitch of Charleston SC
3464 Maybank Highway
☎ 843.557.0401

**Landrum**
Knitter's Nest
101 N. Church Avenue
☎ 864.457.4637

**Lexington**
The Needler
102 E. Main Street
☎ 803.359.3858

**Myrtle Beach**
Knit-N-Purl
4811-B North Kings Highway
☎ 843.945.9484

**North Myrtle Beach**
Knitting up a Storm
1415 Old Highway 17 N.
☎ 843.249.6562

**Orangeburg**
A Stitch-N-Time, Again
1644 Street Matthews Road
☎ 803.534.2612

**Pawleys Island**
Island Knits
10659 Ocean Highway
☎ 843.235.0110

**Seneca**
Piddlin' Patch Craft
& Frame Shoppe
1602 Blue Ridge Boulevard
☎ 864.882.2681

**Summerville**
The Village Knittery
219 S. Cedar Street
☎ 843.261.9276

# South Dakota

**Britton**
Patchworks
1204 5th Street
☎ 605.470.0371

**Groton**
Natural Colored Wool Studio
109 N. 2nd Street
☎ 605.397.4504

**Hot Springs**
Fall River Fibers at Ace Hardware
207 S. Chicago Street
☎ 605.745.5173

**Rapid City**
Dakota Treasures
1215 Mt Rushmore Road
☎ 605.721.9163

**Sioux Falls**
Athena Fibers
3915 S. Hawthorne Avenue
☎ 605.271.0741

**Vermillion**
LumoStudios & Gallery
2 E. Main Street
☎ 605.624.9222

**Watertown**
Expressions Gallery/Knit Nook
1200 9th Avenue SE
☎ 605.886.9251

# Tennessee

**Brentwood**
Bliss Yarns
127 Franklin Road
☎ 615.370.8717

**Charlotte**
Three Creeks Farm
365 Peabody Road
☎ 615.789.5943

**Chattanooga**
Genuine Purl
140 N. Market Street
☎ 423.267.7335

**Cookeville**
T's Yarn Barn
1435 S. Jefferson Avenue
☎ 931.526.6410

**Crossville**
The Yarn Patch
1771 Peavine Road
☎ 931.707.1255

**Dickson**
Yarn Frenzy
107 Myatt Street
☎ 615.446.3577

**Franklin**
The Joy of Knitting
209 S. Royal Oaks Boulevard
Suite 156
☎ 615.925.2745

**Gatlinburg**
Smoky Mountain Spinnery
466 Brookside Village Way
Suite 8
☎ 865.436.9080

**Georgetown**
R & M Yarns
8510 Highway 60
☎ 800.343.9276

**Germantown**
Rainbow Yarn & Fibres
1980 Exeter Road
(In Farmington Centre)
☎ 901.753.9835

**Johnson City**
Yarntiques
410 E. Watauga Avenue
☎ 423.232.2933

**Kingsport**
The Carriage House
528 E. Market Street
☎ 423.247.9091

**Kingston Springs**
Ewe & Company
407 N. Main Street
☎ 615.952.0110

**Knoxville**
Loopville
5204 Kingston Pike
Suite 1
☎ 865.584.9772

The Yarn Haven
464 N. Cedar Bluff Road
☎ 865.694.9900

**Lenoir City**
Forget Me Knot Yarn Shop
2771 Lee Hi Plaza, Highway 11 E.
☎ 865.816.3354

**Memphis**
Yarniverse
709 S. Mendenhall
☎ 901.818.0940

**Monteagle**
Mooney's Market and Emporium
1265 W. Main Street
☎ 931.924.7400

**Murfreesboro**
The Knaughty Knitter
202B N. Thompson Lane
☎ 615.217.4966

**Nashville**
Haus of Yarn
265 White Bridge Road
☎ 615.354.1007

Stitchin' Post
2811 Columbine Place
☎ 615.383.3672

**Rogersville**
Sunny Side Yarns
207 S. Depot Street
☎ 423.272.9276

**Sevierville**
Terri's Yarns & Crafts
927 Dolly Parton Parkway
☎ 865.453.7756

**Signal Mountain**
Three Black Sheep
1229 Taft Highway
☎ 423.886.9276

**Tazewell**
Mountain Hollow Farm Store & Studio
553 Vance Road
☎ 423.869.8927

**Tennessee Ridge**
Yards-N-Yarns
2235 S. Main Street
☎ 931.721.4008

# Texas

**Amarillo**
Stitch 'n Knit
5501 Floyd
☎ 806.355.8811

**Austin**
Gauge Knits
5406 Parkcrest Drive
☎ 512.371.9300

Hill Country Weavers
1701 S. Congress
☎ 512.707.7396

Yarnbow
1310 Ranch Road 620 S.
Suite B-202
☎ 512.666.1310

**Beaumont**
Strings and Things
229 Dowlen Road
☎ 409.225.5185

**Boerne**
Ewe & Eye
512 River Road
☎ 830.249.2083

**Comfort**
Comfort Crockery/
The Loom Room
402 7th Street
☎ 830.995.5299

The Tinsmith's Wife
405 7th Street
☎ 830.995.5539

**Corpus Christi**
Knotty Girl Yarns
5830 McArdle Road, #115
☎ 361.906.9276

**Dallas**
Desert Designs Knitz
5100 Belt Line Rd, #716
☎ 972.392.9276

Holley's Yarn Shoppe
5211 Forest Lane
Suite 115
☎ 972.503.5648

White Rock Weaving
1212 Tavaros Avenue
☎ 214.320.9276

Yarn and Stitches
15615 Coit Road
Suite 206
☎ 972.239.9665

**El Paso**
Mayaluna Yarns
5024 Doniphan Drive
Suite 10
☎ 915.585.7779

Mundo De Papel
3417 Alameda Avenue
☎ 915.351.0250

Sarita's Custom Sewing
5857 N. Mesa Street
Suite 12
☎ 915.581.6586

**Farmersville**
Fiber Circle
200 McKinny Street
☎ 972.782.6630

**Ft. Worth**
Jenning Street Yarns
217 S. Jennings Avenue
☎ 817.878.2740

Madtosh
4119 Camp Bowie Boulevard
Suite 121
☎ 817.420.9366

**Friendswood**
Marie's Yarn Shop
210 Dawn Street
☎ 281.482.8546

**Georgetown**
Fiber Arts Republic
170 Young Ranch Road
☎ 512.868.8695

Needlearts of Georgetown
708 S. Rock Street
☎ 512.869.2182

**Granbury**
Yarn Extraordinaire
214 N. Crockett Street
☎ 817.707.1012

**Grandview**
Heritage Arts
10740 County Road #102
☎ 817.866.2772

**Grand Prairie**
Knitting Fairy
2100 TX 360 #1904
☎ 214.412.2889

**Horseshoe Bay**
Nan's Needleworks
100 Bunny Run Lane #205
☎ 830.598.4560

**Houston**
Knitting in the Loop
2801 Bammel Lane
☎ 713.942.7881

Merribee Needlearts
12682 Shiloh Church Road
☎ 281.440.6980

Nancy's Knits
5300 N. Braeswood Boulevard
☎ 713.661.9411

Nimblefingers
12456 Memorial Drive
☎ 713.722.7244

**Jonestown**
Happy Ewe
18360 Farm to Market 1431
☎ 512.284.7408

**Katy**
Yarntopia
2944 S. Mason Road
☎ 281.392.2386

**Killeen**
Old Spinning Wheel Yarn Shop
10540 State Highway 195
☎ 254.526.YARN

**La Grange**
The Quilted Skein
126 W. Colorado Street
☎ 979.968.8200

**Lancaster**
The Sassy Spinster
129 Historic Town Square
☏ 972.218.5335

**League City**
Park Avenue Yarns
260 Park Avenue
☏ 832.932.0300

**Longview**
Stitches 'n Stuff
7793 N. Highway 259
☏ 903.663.3840

**Lytle**
Pyron's
15126 Main Street
☏ 830.709.4055

**McAllen**
The Lamb's Loom
1209 Pecan Boulevard
☏ 956.607.6855

**Midland**
Stitching Post
4610 N. Garfield Street
Suite B4
☏ 432.697.1241

**Navasota**
WC Mercantile
201 E. Washington Avenue
☏ 936.825.3378

**Paige**
Yarnorama
130 Gonzales Street
☏ 512.253.0100

**Plano**
Threads that Bind
3100 Independence Parkway
#204/205
☏ 972.867.5700

**Port Lavaca**
Beefore It's A Quilt
119 E. Main Street
☏ 361.552.1350

**Rockport**
Golden Needles & Quilts
701 N. Allen Street
☏ 361.729.7873

**Salado**
The Salado Yarn Co.
22 N. Main Street
(Southern Comforts Bldg)
☏ 254.947.0595

**San Angelo**
Chandler Cottage
1821 Knickerbocker Road
Suite E
☏ 325.227.6985

The Fiber Co-op
7024 Orient Road
☏ 325.262.5447

**San Antonio**
Inskein Yarns
8425 Bandera Road
Suite 128
☏ 210.334.0200

Unraveled
815 E. Rector
Suite 104A
☎ 210.251.4451

Yarnivore
2357 NW Military Highway
☎ 210.979.8255

**Seguin**
You're So Crafty
107 N. Camp Street
☎ 830.379.0730

**Spring**
Twisted Yarns
702 Spring Cypress Drive
Suite A
☎ 281.528.8664

**Texarkana**
The Yarn Garden
3423 New Boston Road
☎ 903.223.9276

**The Woodlands**
iPurl
3335 College Park Drive
Suite 450
☎ 936.242.1031

**Tyler**
Granny's Needle Haus
6004 S. Broadway Avenue
☎ 903.561.4637

Rose Path Weaving
13161 County Road 461
☎ 903.882.3234

**Wimberley**
Ply Yarn Art
Quarter Shops on Cypress Creek
14015 RR 12
Suite #4
☎ 512.406.1719

# Utah

**Bountiful**
Hemstitched Heirlooms
585 W. 2600 S.
☎ 801.298.8212

**Cedar City**
The Yarn Bard
97 W-400 South Street
☎ 435.531.8789

**Centerville**
Judy's Novelty Wool
1035 N. Main Street
☎ 801.298.1356

**Clearfield**
Sew-N- Save
1475 S. State
Suite A
☎ 801.825.2177

**Delta**
Mom's Crafts and Fabrics
313 S. 100 W.
☎ 435.864.3325

**Ferron**
Pat's Sew N' Stuff
35 E. Main Street
☎ 435.384.2620

**Moab**
Desert Thread
29 E. Center Street
☎ 435.259.8404

**Ogden**
Knit Craft Studio
432 27th Street
☎ 801.394.9304

Needlepoint Joint
241 Historic 25th Street
☎ 801.394.4355

**Provo**
Heindselman's Yarn Needlework
176 W. Center Street
☎ 801.373.5193

**Richfield**
Julia's Shoppe
330 S. 100 E.
☎ 435.896.1821

**Salt Lake City**
Blazing Needles
1365 S. 1100 E.
☎ 801.487.5648

Piper's Quilts & Comforts
1944 S. 1100 E.
☎ 801.484.5890

Wool Cabin
2020 E. 3300 S.
☎ 801.466.1811

**Sandy**
Daines Cotton Shops
9441 S. 700 E.
☎ 801.572.1412

Gingerbread Antiques and Yarn
8540 S. 700 E.
☎ 801.255.5666

The Handmaiden
16 E. Main Street
☎ 801.566.6350

Unraveled Sheep
9316 S. 700 E.
☎ 801.255.6833

**Tooele**
Yard Sale Fabrics & Gifts
60 S. Main Street
☎ 435.843.0139

**West Jordan**
Kamille's
1100 W. 7800 S.
Bldg. #6
☎ 801.282.0477

Knittin' Pretty
1393 W. 9000 S.
☎ 801.676.9933

# Vermont

**Bennington**
The Scarlett Creation
493 Main Street
☎ 802.447.3794

**Brattleboro**
Knit or Dye
41 Main Street
☎ 802.258.9100

Hand Knits
56 Elliot Street
☎ 802.579.1799

**Burlington**
Creative Habitat
555 Shelburne Road
☎ 802.862.0646

**Dorset**
Black Sheep Yarns
VT Route 30 & Stonewall Lane
☎ 802.362.2411

**Dover**
Ugly Duckling Yarn
114 Route 100
☎ 802.464.6300

**Manchester Center**
Yarns for Your Soul
605 Depot Street
☎ 802.362.3151

**Middlebury**
Cacklin' Hens
383 Exchange Street
☎ 802.388.2221

**Montpelier**
The Knitting Studio
112 Main Street
☎ 802.229.2444

**Montgomery Center**
Mountain Fiber Folk Cooperative
188 Main Street
☎ 802.326.2092

**Morrisville**
Bailey House Floral and Greenhouses
853 Brooklyn Street
☎ 802.888.7909

**Newport**
Ewe Forium
79 Coventry Street
☎ 802.334.9955

**Norwich**
Northern Nights Yarn Shop
Corner of Main Street and Elm Street
☎ 802.649.2000

**Poultney**
Stitchy Women
150 Main Street
☎ 802.287.4114

**Proctorsville**
Six Loose Ladies
7 Depot Street
☎ 802.226.7373

**Putney**
Green Mountain Spinnery
1 Brickyard Lane
☎ 802.387.4528

**Rutland**
Green Mountain Fibers Yarn Store
259 Woodstock Avenue
☎ 802.775.7800

**Springfield**
Baker's
41 Chester Road
☎ 802.885.3446

**Stowe**
Stowe Fabric & Yarn
37 Depot Street
☎ 802.253.6740

**Waitsfield**
Shades of Winter Yarn Shop
5123 Main Street, Route 100
☎ 802.496.9040

**White River Junction**
White River Yarns
49 South Main Street
☎ 802.295.9301

**Williston**
Northeast Fiber Arts Center
7531 Williston Road
☎ 802.288.8081

**Woodstock**
Whippletree Yarn Shop
7 Central Street
☎ 802.457.1325

# Virginia

**Abingdon**
A Likely Yarn
213 Pecan Street
☎ 276.628.2143

**Alexandria**
In Stitches
8800 F Pear Tree Court
☎ 703.360.4600

Fibre Space
1219 King Street
☎ 703.664.0344

**Blacksburg**
Mosaic Yarn Shop
880 University City Boulevard
☎ 540.961.4462

The New River Fiber Co.
880 University City Boulevard
☎ 540.552.0231

**Burke**
The Yarn Barn
9413-C Old Burke Lake Road
☎ 703.978.2220

**Charlottesville**
Laughing Sheep Yarns
188 Zan Road
☎ 804.973.0331

Mangham Wool and
Mohair Farm
901 Hammocks Gap Road
☎ 434.973.2222

The Needle Lady
111 West Main Street
☎ 434.296.4625

Stony Mountain Fibers
939 Hammocks Gap Road
☎ 434.295.2008

**Chincoteague Island**
Carodan Farm Wool Shop
357 Maddox Boulevard
☎ 800.985.7083

### Churchville
Cestari Sheep & Wool Company
3581 Churchville Avenue
☎ 540.337.7282

### Culpeper
Dog House Yarns and More
708 Sunset Lane
☎ 540.825.3585

### Dillwyn
Kirtland's Yarn Barn
5077 Andersonville Road
☎ 800.850.6008

### Fairfax
Nature's Yarns
11212 Lee Highway
☎ 703.273.3596

### Falls Church
Aylins Woolgatherer
7245 Arlington Boulevard
Suite 318
☎ 703.573.1900

### Fancy Gap
Peaceful Heart Alpacas
Farm & Store
1563 Misty Trail
☎ 276.728.4950

### Floyd
Schoolhouse Fabrics
220 N. Locust Street
☎ 540.745.4561

Woolly Jumper Yarns
202 S. Locust Street
☎ 540.745.5648

### Fredericksburg
Knit 2 Unwind
5320 Plank Road
☎ 540.786.2092

Old Town Yarnery
433 Elm Street
☎ 540.373.9276

### Gloucester Courthouse
Coordinated Colors Yarn Shoppe
6651 Main Street
☎ 804.824.9026

### Haymarket
Needles In The Haymarket
15125 Washington St. #108
☎ 703.659.1062

### Hot Springs
Passion-Knit Living Studios
5620 Hot Springs Road
☎ 540.962.7557

### Leesburg
Cutthroat Yarn
1609 Village Market Boulevard
SE #115
☎ 703.771.0100

### Lexington
Saville Hill Farm & Studio
140 Lacy Lane
☎ 540.463.5471

### Lynchburg
Backstitches
100 Wayne Drive
☎ 434.385.0185

Suzanne's Knitting Shoppe
2820 Linkhorne Drive
☎ 434.384.7114

### Norfolk
Baa Baa Sheep
754 West 22nd Street
☎ 757.802.9229

### Onancock
Purls
6 North Street
☎ 757.787.2277

### The Plains
Hunt Country Yarns
6482 Main Street
☎ 540.253.9990

### Radford
Sew Biz
92 & 94 Harvey Street
☎ 540.639.1138

### Raphine
Orchardside Yarn Shop
273 Raphine Road
☎ 540.348.5220

### Richmond
The Knitting Basket
5812 Grove Avenue
☎ 804.282.2909

### Roanoke
Mosaic Yarn Shop 3117
Franklin Road SW
☎ 540.685.2285

Yarn Explosion
5227 Airport Road NW
☎ 540.206.2638

### Rocky Mount
The Crooked Stitch Quilts
and Knits
375 Franklin Street
☎ 540.420.7129

### Sperryvilles
Knit Wit Yarn Shop
12018 Lee Highway
☎ 540.987.8251

### Suffolk
Serendipity Farm & Studio
980 Cypress Chapel Road
☎ 757.986.2010

### Vienna
Uniquities
421D Church Street NE
☎ 703.242.0520

### Virginia Beach
Knit Wits
945 Providence Square
Shopping Center
☎ 757.495.6600

The Yarn Club
240 Mustang Trail
Suite 8
☎ 757.486.5648

### Warrenton
The Red Thread
10 S. 5th Street
☎ 540.878.2039

**Waynesboro**
JJ's Knitting Knook
3396 Stuarts Draft Highway
☎ 540.337.3770

**Williamsburg**
Knitting Sisters
1915 Pocahontas Trail
Suite B1
☎ 757.258.5005

**Winchester**
Knit 1, Purl 2
20 W. Boscawen Street
☎ 540.662.6098

Never Enough Yarn
393 Millwood Avenue
☎ 540.665.1800

**Woodbridge**
Yarn Cloud
13895 Hedgewood Drive
Suite 113
☎ 703.763.3285

**Wytheville**
Wythe Yarn
175 A-B N. Tazewell Street
☎ 276.223.4459

**Yorktown**
Coordinated Colors Yarn Shoppe
4320 George Washington Memorial Highway
☎ 757.874.3939

# Washington

**Allyn**
Allyn Knit Shop & Spinning Supply
16590 Highway 3
☎ 360.275.4729

**Anacortes**
Ana Cross Stitch
713 Commercial Avenue
☎ 360.299.9010

**Bainbridge Island**
Churchmouse Yarns & Teas
118 Madrone Lane N.
☎ 206.780.2686

**Birch Bay**
Beach Basket Yarn and Gifts
7620 Birch Bay Drive
☎ 360.371.0332

**Bothell**
Mad Cow Yarns
18107 Bothell Way NE
☎ 425.415.6981

Yarn of Eden
826 237th Street SE
☎ 425.492.4744

**Bellingham**
Apple Yarns
1780 Iowa Street
☎ 360.756.9992

NW Handspun Yarns
1401 Commercial Street
☎ 360.738.0167

Wool Station
1103 11th Street
☎ 360.671.4031

**Buckley**
Elizabeth's Fiber & Yarn
24912 112th Street E.
☎ 253.267.9870

**Carnation**
Tolt Yarn and Wool
4509 Tolt Avenue
☎ 425.333.4066

**Cashmere**
Cashmere Cottage Yarn
102A Maple Street
☎ 509.782.0382

**Chehalis**
Yarn & Things
545 North Market #5
☎ 360.748.2134

**Chelan**
Twisted Fine Yarn and Wool
210 E. Woodin
☎ 509.888.0285

**Cle Elum**
Ruby's Printing, Scrapbooking & Things
E.1st Street
☎ 509.674.2296

**Clarkston**
Patrick's Craft Shop
840 6th Street
☎ 509.758.2110

**Clinton**
Paradise Found Fiber Farm
4081 Springwater Lane
☎ 360.579.1906

**Colville**
E.Z. Knit
165 N. Main Street
☎ 509.684.2644

**Coupeville**
Whidbey Isle Yarns, Gifts and Teas
302 N. Main Street #D
☎ 360.632.4200

**Dayton**
Jacci's Yarn Basket
242 E. Main Street
☎ 509.382.2526

**Deer Park**
In Stitches
206 S. Main Street
☎ 509.276.2244

**Des Moines**
All Points Yarn
21921 Marine View Drive S.
☎ 206.824.YARN

**Duvall**
Quintessential Knits
26401 NE Richardson Street
☎ 425.890.6756

**Eatonville**
The Country Mouse
755 Eatonville Highway W.
☎ 360.832.8065

Reflection Farm Sheep & Wool Products
31801 79th Avenue, Court E.
☎ 253.380.5511

**Ellensburg**
Yarn Folk
304 North Pearl Street
☎ 509.304.4588

**Friday Harbor**
Island Wools
140 B First Street
☎ 360.370.5648

**Gig Harbor**
Rainy Day Yarns
3200 Tarabochia Street
☎ 253.514.6890

Great Yarns
4023 Rucker Avenue
☎ 425.252.8155

**Grayland**
Yarn N. Darn Things
2172 Highway 105
☎ 360.267.0281

**Ilwaco**
Purly Shell Fiber Arts
157 Howerton Street
Suite B
☎ 360.642.3044

**Kelso**
LaFavorites
204 S. Pacific Avenue
☎ 360.575.9305

**Kennewick**
Sheep's Clothing
8551 Gage Boulevard
Suite H
☎ 509.734.2484

**Kent**
Makers' Mercantile
18437 E. Valley Highway
☎ 425.251.1239

**Kirkland**
Serial Knitters
8427 122nd Ave NE
☎ 425.242.0086

**La Conner**
Jennings Yarn & Needlecrafts
104 S. 1st Street
☎ 206.466.3177

**Lakewood**
Yorkshire Yarns
6122 Motor Avenue SE
☎ 253.589.YARN

**Langley**
Knitty Purls
111 Anthes Avenue
☎ 360.331.2212

**Lopez Island**
Island Fibers
4208 Port Stanley Road
☎ 360.468.2467 by appt. only

**Lynden**
Wear on Earth
504 Front Street
☎ 360.318.8657

**Mt. Vernon**
WildFibers
706 S. 1st Street
☎ 360.336.5202

**Ocean Park**
Tapestry Rose
1024 Bay Avenue
☎ 360.665.5385

**Olympia**
Canvas Works
525 Columbia Street SW
☎ 360.352.4481

**Port Angeles**
Cabled Fiber Studio
125 W. 1st Street
☎ 360.504.2233

**Port Gamble**
The Artful Ewe
32180 Rainier Avenue NE
☎ 360.643.0183

**Port Orchard**
A Good Yarn Shop
1140 Bethel Avenue
☎ 360.876.0377

**Port Townsend**
Bazaar Girls Yarn Shop
126 Quincy Street
☎ 360.379.9273

Diva Yarn
940 Water Street
☎ 360.385.4844

**Renton**
The Knittery
601 S. Grady Way
Suite C
☎ 425.228.4694

**Seattle**
Bad Woman Yarn
1815 N. 45th Street
Suite 215
☎ 206.547.5384

The Fiber Gallery
8212 Greenwood Avenue N.
☎ 206.706.4197

Little Knits
3200 Airport Way S.
Bldg 8, Suite 110
☎ 206.935.4072

Seattle Yarn
5633 California SW
☎ 206.935.2010

So Much Yarn
1525 First Avenue, #4
☎ 206.443.0727

Stitches
711 E. Pike Street
☎ 206.709.0707

The Tea Cozy Yarn Shop
5816 24th Avenue NW
☎ 206.783.3322

Tricoter
3121 E. Madison Street
☎ 206.328.6505

The Weaving Works
4717 Brooklyn Avenue NE
☎ 206.524.1221

**Sequim**
A Dropped Stitch
136 S. 2nd Avenue
☎ 360.582.1410

**Shelton**
Fancy Image Yarn
SE 591 Arcadia Road
☎ 360.426.5875

**Snohomish**
Country Yarns
119 Avenue B
☎ 360.568.7611

**Spokane**
A Grand Yarn
1220 S. Grand Boulevard
☎ 509.455.8213

A Heart like Yours Quilt Shoppe
9212 E. Montgomery
Suite 202
☎ 509.924.1020

Paradise Fibers
225 W. Indiana
☎ 888.320.7746

Sew E-Z Too
603 W. Garland
☎ 509.325.6644

**Stanwood**
Pinchknitter Yarns
8712 271st Street
☎ 360.939.0769

**Tacoma**
Fibers Etc.
705 Court C
☎ 253.572.1859

**Toppenish**
Hope Chest Crafts
508 W. Second Avenue
☎ 509.865.5666

**Twisp**
Twisted Knitters
502 South Glover Street
☎ 509.997.0233

**Vashon**
Island Quilter
17639 Vashon Highway SW
☎ 206.713.6000

Vashon Pharmacy
17617 Vashon Highway SW
☎ 206.463.9118

**Washougal**
Woolly Woolly Wagtails Yarns
982 E. Street
☎ 360.835.9649

**Wenatchee**
Elite Needlework Shoppe
205 N. Chelan
☎ 509.662.9773

**Yelm**
Gee Gee's Quilting, Inc.
601 W. Yelm Avenue
☎ 360.458.5616

# West Virginia

**Bridgeport**
The Nest
601 S. Virginia
☎ 304.848.2444

**Charleston**
Kanawha City Yarn Co.
5132-A MacCorkle Avenue SE
☎ 304.926.8589

**Elkins**
Yarn and Company
Airport/Country Club Road Rt4
☎ 304.636.3760

**Lewisburg**
O'Shea's All About Beauty
129 W. Washington Street
☎ 304.645.3500

**Morgantown**
The Needlecraft Barn
162 Chancery Row
☎ 304.296.3789

**Parkersburg**
Market Street Yarn and Crafts
615 Market Street
☎ 304.865.9276

**Reedsville**
Eleanor's Quilts & Fabrics
399 North Robert Stone Way
☎ 304.864.6330

**Shepherdstown**
Yarnability
207 S. Princess
☎ 304.876.8081

**Sistersville**
Quintilla's Fabrics
815 Gold Ring Road
☎ 304.758.2890

**Sutton**
The Needle Basket
208 Main Street
☎ 304.765.7505

# Wisconsin

**Argyle**
Argyle Fiber Mill
200 E. Milwaukee Street
☎ 608.543.3933

**Antigo**
The Cutting Edge
816 5th Avenue
☎ 715.623.3590

**Appleton**
Iris Fine Yarns
132 East Wisconsin Avenue
☎ 920.954.9001

**Ashland**
The Craft Connection
205 Main Street East
☎ 715.682.6454

Northwoods Dyeworks
417B Main Street W.
☎ 715.682.0588

**Bayfield**
Brownstone Centre
121 Rittenhouse Avenue
☎ 715.779.5571

**Beaver Dam**
Firefly Fibers
112 Front Street
☎ 920.356.8859

**Beloit**
Attic Quilts
322 State Street
☎ 608.364.4037

**Brookfield**
Cream City Yarn
15565 W. North Avenue
☎ 262.923.7014

River Boutique and Yarn
18900 W. Bluemound Road
☎ 262.641.7427

**Burlington**
Artistic Fibers
324 N. Pine Street
☎ 262.757.0960

**Cambridge**
Kaleidoscope Fibers
131 West Main Street
☎ 920.342.0496

**Cedar Grove**
Bahr Creek Llamas & Fiber Studio
N.1021 Sauk Trail Road
☎ 920.668.6417

**Chetek**
Elly's Sheared Sheep Yarn & Fabric Shop
602 2nd Street
Center Court Building
☎ 715.925.9276

**Columbus**
Susan's Fiber Shop
N250 County Road A
☎ 920.623.4237

**Delafield**
Knitch
608 Milwaukee Street
☎ 262.646.9392

**Delavan**
Needles 'n Pins Yarn Shoppe
W9034 County Road A
Richmond
☎ 608.883.9922

Studio S
W.8903 Country Road A
☎ 608.883.2123

**East Troy**
Linda's Yarns
2075 Division Street
☎ 262.642.5205

**Ettrick**
Christa's Yarn & Crafts
W14271 County Road C
☎ 608.525.2757

**Evansville**
The Dancing Lamb
17 W. Main Street
☎ 608.882.0267

**Fond du Lac**
The Knitting Room
28 N. Main Street
☎ 920.906.4800

**Fox Point**
Knitting Knook
6858 N. Santa Monica Boulevard
☎ 414.540.4080

**Frederic**
Fibre Functions Yarns
682 263rd Avenue
☎ 715.472.8276

**Gordon**
Kunert Kreations
9586 E. County Road Y
☎ 715.376.4722

**Grafton**
Grafton Yarn Store
1300 14th Avenue
☎ 262.377.0344

**Green Bay**
Patti's Yarn Shop
1512 Main Street
☎ 920.433.9276

**Hartford**
Main Street Yarn Shop
59 N. Main Street
☎ 262.673.2203

Sheeping Beauty Fibre Arts
W533 State Road 33
☎ 262.623.0244

**Horicon**
Knitty Gritty Shop
W5346 State Road 33
☎ 920.485.0549

**Janesville**
Dragon Fly
1327 N. Wright Road
☎ 608.757.9228

**Kaukauna**
Make Do
127 W. Wisconsin (inside KC&T)
☎ 920.766.4038

**Kenosha**
Fiddlehead Yarns
7511 26th Avenue
☎ 262.925.6487

**La Crosse**
Baskets of Yarn
2026 Rose Court
☎ 608.783.1402

Fitting Knit Shop
533 Main Street
☎ 608.784.4920

**Madison**
The Knitting Tree
2636 Monroe Street
☎ 608.238.0121

Stitchers Crossing
6122 Mineral Point Road
☎ 608.232.1500

Wisconsin Craft Market
148 Westgate Mall
☎ 608.271.6002

**Milton**
Loose Threads
8005 N. Milton Road
State Road 26
☎ 608.868.7912

**Milwaukee**
Fiberwood Studio Ltd.
2709 N. 92nd St
☎ 414.302.1849

The Knitting Knook
6858 N. Santa Monica Boulevard
☎ 414.540.4080

Midwest Yarn
3385 S. Kinnickinnic Ave
☎ 414.979.9276

**Monroe**
Orange Kitten Yarns
1620 11th Street
☎ 608.328.4140

**Montello**
Teapot Quilt Cottage
505 Main Street
☎ 608.297.7849

**Neenah**
Yarns by Design
123 W. Wisconsin Avenue
☎ 920.727.0530

**Nekoosa**
Knitwise Yarns and
Fiber Arts Gallery
421 County Road G
☎ 715.886.1030

**New Richmond**
Doyle's Farm & Home
560 Deere Drive
☎ 715.246.6184

**Omro**
YDS
5530 State Road 116
☎ 920.582.7196

**Osceola**
Mrs. I's Yarn Parlor
101 Cascade Street
☎ 715.494.0385

**Racine**
Sew 'n Save
3701 Durand Avenue
☎ 262.554.8708

**Ripon**
Bungalow Quilting and Yarn
646 W. Fond Du Lac Street
☎ 920.517.1910

**Roberts**
Color Crossing
201 N. Vine Street
☎ 715.749.3337

**Sheboygan Falls**
Magpie's Cottage
308 Pine Street
☎ 920.467.9978

**St. Germain**
Sutter's Gold'n Fleece
9094 County Road O
☎ 715.479.7634

**Solon Springs**
The Little Gift House
9234 E. Main Street
☎ 715.378.4170

**Spooner**
Northwind Book & Fiber
205 Walnut Street
☎ 715.635.6811

**Sturgeon Bay**
Spin
108 S. Madison Avenue
☎ 920.746.7746

**Sun Prairie**
Prairie Junction Yarn
227 E. Main Street
☎ 608.837.8909

**Superior**
Fabric Works
1320 Tower Avenue
☎ 715.392.7060

**Tomah**
Bear Creek Fibers
27686 Holly Avenue
☎ 608.374.4078

**Two Rivers**
Intertwined
1623 Washington Street
☎ 920.629.9011

**Verona**
The Sow's Ear
125 S. Main Street
☎ 608.848.2755

**Viroqua**
Ewetopia Fiber Shop
122 S. Main Street
☎ 608.637.3443

**Washington Island**
Sievers School of Fiber Arts
Jackson Harbor Road
☎ 920.847.2264

**Wausau**
Black Purl
1102 3rd Street
☎ 715.843.7875

**West Bend**
Xpressions Yarn
& Bead Boutique
264 N. Main Street
☎ 262.306.1300

**Weyauwega**
The Knitting Nest
103 W. Main Street
☎ 920.862.0111

**Whitehall**
Renee's Stitchery & Boutique
36237 West Street
☎ 715.538.2238

**Woodruff**
Hidden Talents
9404 County Highway J
☎ 715.358.3787

# Wyoming

**Afton**
The Cottage
419 Washington Street
☎ 307.885.2522

**Casper**
Dancing Sheep Yarn and Fiber
E. 2nd Street
☎ 307.265.6173

**Cheyenne**
Ewe Count
819 Randall Avenue
☎ 307.638.1148

**Douglas**
The Prairie Stitcher
120 N. 3rd Street
☎ 307.358.5571

**Evanston**
Common Threads Quilting
1029 Main Street
☎ 307.444.1675

R & V Sewing & High Country Fabric
1129 Main Street
☎ 307.389.7300

**Gillette**
Crazy Woman Mercantile
214 S. Gillette Avenue
☎ 307.682.3152

**Green River**
Keama's Quilts
91 W. Flaming Gorge
☎ 307.875.5461

**Jackson**
Knit On Pearl
145 W. Gill Avenue
☎ 307.733.5648

**Laramie**
Cowgirl Yarn
119 Ivinson Avenue
☎ 307.755.9276

Jeny Originals Yarns and Handwovens
213 Grand Avenue
☎ 307.742.7597

Woobee KnitShop
10 Knoll Drive
☎ 307.760.2092

**Pinedale**
Heritage Quilts & Fabric Shoppe
21 E. Pine Street
☎ 307.367.7397

**Powell**
Cut & Sew Fabrics
217 N. Bent Street
☎ 307.754.7247

**Rock Springs**
Willow Ridge Crafts
421 N. Front Street
☎ 307.362.2556

**Sheridan**
The Fiber House
146 Coffeen Avenue
☎ 307.673.0383

**Torrington**
The Doll Factory
2006 Main Street
☎ 307.532.4151

# Canada

## Alberta

**Blairmore**
A Nest of Needles Wool Shop
12921 - 20 Avenue
T0K 0E0
☎ 403.564.4041

**Edmonton**
MacPhee Workshop
Box 10, Site 16, RR 8
T5L 4H8
☎ 780.973.3516 (call first)

River City Yarns
16956 111th Avenue, NW
T5M 4C9
☎    780.477.9276

**Calgary**
Gina Brown's
5718 1A St. SW #107
T2H 0E8
☎ 403.255.2200

Pudding Yarn
1516 6th Street SW
T2R 0Z8
☎ 403.244.2996

STASH Needle Art Lounge
1309 9 Avenue SE
AB T2G 0T3
☎ 403.457.0766

## British Columbia

**Langley**
88 Stitches
21183 88th Avenue #602
V1M 2G5
☎ 604.888.6689

**North Vancouver**
Urban Yarns Edgemont Village
3111 Highland Boulevard
V7R 2X5
☎ 604.984.2214

**Port Moody**
Black Sheep Yarns
88 Grant Street
V3H 2B7
☎ 778.355.9665

**Vernon**
A Twist of Yarn
3915 31st Street
☎ 250.549.4200

## Manitoba

**Brandon**
The Knit2Scrap2 Store
215 6th Street – Unit 1
R7A 3N3
☎ 204.717.5272

**Winnipeg**
Ram Wools Yarn Co-op
989 Portage Avenue
R3G 0R7
☎ 204.949.6868

# New Brunswick

**Bathurst**
Spinning Wheel Yarn Shop
309 King Avenue
E2A 1P4
☎ 506.549.4367

**Blacks Harbour**
Cricket Cove Fine Handknits
836 Main Street
E0G 1H0
☎ 506.456.3897

**Harvey York County**
Briggs & Little Woolen Mills
3500 Route 635
E6K 1J8
☎ 800.561.9276

**Lakeburn**
London-Wul Farm
1937 Melanson Road
E1H 2C6
☎ 506.382.6990

**St. Andrews**
Cottage Crafts Tweeds & Yarns
209 Water Street
E5B 1B3
☎ 506.814.0054

# Newfoundland

**Saint John's**
CAST ON! CAST OFF!
685 Water Street
A1E 1B5
☎ 709.739.7318

Nonia
286 Water Street
NL A1C 1B8
☎ 709.753.8062

# Nova Scotia

**Baddeck**
Baadeck Yarns
16 Chebucto Street
☎ 877.707.5512

**Dartmouth**
Atlantic Fabrics
Staples Plaza
114 Woodlawn Road
☎ 902.434.7220

**Halifax**
The Loop
1547 Barrington Street
B3J 1Z4
☎ 902.429.5667

**Mabou**
Bellemeade Farm
166 Rankinville Road
Cape Breton Island
(by appt. only)
☎ 902.945.2256

**Pictou**
Water Street Studio Co-Op
110 Water Street
B0K 1H0
☎ 902.485.8398

# Ontario

**Almonte**
Textile Traditions
87 Mill Street
K0A 1A0
☎ 613.256.3907

**Ashburn**
Myrtle Station Wool
& Ferguson's Knitting
9585 Baldwin Street
L0B 1A0
☎ 905.655.4858

**Aurora**
Needles & Knits
15040 Yonge Street
L4G 1N4
☎ 905.713.2066

**Barrie**
Eliza's Button's & Yarn
250 Bayview Drive
L4N 4Y8
☎ 705.725.8536

**Belleville**
G & G Handcrafts
1863B Old Hwy #2
K8N 4Z2
☎ 613.968.4221

**Bracebridge**
Muskoka Yarn Connection
295 Wellington Street, Unit 12
P1L 1P3
☎ 705.645.5819

**Brighton**
Robbin's Nest
53 Main Street
K0K 1H0
☎ 613.475.0578

**Cambridge**
Cambridge Fibres
215 Queen Street West
N3C 1G6
☎ 519.658.8237

**Elora**
Yarn Bird
22 Mill Street West
N0B 1S0
☎ 519.846.0003

**Essex**
Knit One Purl One
8 Talbot Street N.
N8M 1A4
☎ 519.776.8262

**Guelph**
All Strung Out 36
Quebec Street
N1H 2T4
☎ 226.820.3766

**Hamilton**
Cardiknits
92 Cardinal Drive
L9A 4H7
☎ 905.389.9336

Handknit Yarn Studio
144 James Street N.
L8R 2K7
☎ 905.393.5976

**Kenora**
Painted Sheep Boutique
314 1st Avenue S.
P9N 1W7
☎ 807.468.4399

**Kingston**
Wool-Tyme Kingston
725 Gardiners Road
K7M 3Y5
☎ 613.384.3951

**Lakefield**
Eleanor's Yarns & Books
44 Queen Street
K0L 2H0
☎ 705.652.7535

**Lindsay**
Aberdeen's Wool Company
228 Kent Street West
Kawartha Lakes
K9V 2Z2
☎ 705.928.5417

# Niagara Falls Area

**Fonthill/Pelham**
Rose's Fine Yarns
67 Canboro Road
L0S 1E0
☎ 905.892.2222

**Niagara on the Lake/Virgil**
Modern Bee
1507 Niagara Stone Road
L0S 1T0
☎ 905.468.8190

**Otonabee**
A River of Yarn
353 Kent's Bay Road
K0L 2G0
☎ 705.740.3881

**Ottawa**
Wabi Sabi
1078 Wellington Street W.
K1Y 2Y3
☎ 613.725.5648

Yarn Forward & Sew-On
581 Bank Street
☎ 613.237.8008

**Picton**
Rose Haven Farm Store
187 Picton Main Street
K0K 2T0
☎ 613.476.9092

**Port Moody**
Black Sheep Yarns
88 Grant Street
V3H 0B6
☎ 778.355.9665

**Stratford**
Alpaca Acres Farm Store
3979 Road 108
N5A 6S5
☎ 519.625.1064

## Toronto

Alpaca Avenue
1128 Martin Grove Road
M9W 4W1
☎ 416.357.1169

Americo Original
456 Queen Street West
M5V 2A8
☎ 416.777.9747

Knitomatic
1378 Bathurst Street
M5R 3J1
☎ 416.653.7849

Lettuce Knit
86 Nassau Street
M5T 1M5
☎ 416.203.9970

## Windsor

Knit One Sew Too
3703 Walker Road
N8W 3S9
☎ 519.966.7444

# Prince Edward Island

## Bloomfield

MacAusland's Woolen Mill
RR #2, 150 Bloomfield
C0B 1E0
☎ 902.859.3005

## Borden-Carleton

Julie's Yarn Shoppe
23524 Trans-Canada Highway
C0B 1X0
☎ 902.437.3098

## North Rustico

North Shore Island Traditions
7176 Main Street
C0A 1X0
☎ 902.963.2453

# Quebec

## Quebec City

Effiloché
6260 Rue Saint-Hubert
QC H2S 2M2
☎ 514.276.2547

La Bobineuse de Laine
2196 Avenue du Mont Royal East
QC H2H 1K3
☎ 514.521.9000

La Maison Tricotée
751 rue Gilford
QC H2J 1N8
☎ 514.903.9665

## Salaberry de Valleyfield

Amitié et Passion
18 Nicholson
QC J6T 4M3
☎ 450.370.1001

## Ste. Adèle

Au P'tit Brin De Laine
1332, Suite 100
Boulevard Ste.Adèle
QC J8B 1A8
☎ 450.229.2221

**St-Bruno-de-Montarville**
Biscotte & Cie
1315, Rue Roberval
QC J3V 5J1
☎ 450.482.1513

# Saskatchewan

**Moose Jaw**
Stitcher's Nook
50 Stadacona St W
S6H 1Z1
☎ 306.692.5377

**Prince Albert**
Beth's Yarn & Needle Craft
Boutique
909A Central Avenue
S6V 4V2
☎ 306.764.6910

# Yukon

**Whitehorse**
Itsy-Bitsy Yarn Store
Unit 125-1116 Front Street
Y1A 1A3
☎ 867.689.9720

# Mexico

**(The country code for Mexico is 52)**
**Yarn=Hilo**

## Nuevo Leon

**Monterrey**
El Niágara del Norte, S.A.
José María Morelos y Pavón
555 Col. Centro
☎ 52.8342.4023

**San Pedro Garza García**
Crochet
Av. Manuel Gomez Morín
911-7 Col. Del Valle
☎ 52.8335.2980

## Jalisco

**Zapopan**
Estambres de Silvia
Plaza Universidad Local C-4
(Av. Patria esq. Pablo Neruda)
45120
☎ 52.36.10.18.02

Estambres de Silvia Av.
Niño Obrero #699-A
(Casi esq. Av. Tepeyac)
45050 Zapopan
☎ 52.33.3123.0295

## Tecate

Dora's Knitting
Ave 6 #90 PTE
21400
☎ 665.654.5672

# The Caribbean

Often difficult to find in the Caribbean, specialty yarn shops are rarely seen. The shops listed below are not necessarily specialty shops, but rather craft shops with some yarn and other supplies.

## Aruba

**(The country code for Arubas is 297)**

The Craft Shop
Tanki Leendert 241
☎ 297.587.8272

## Barbados

**(The country code for Barbados is 246)**

**Bridgetown**
Laurie Dash and Sons
The Craft shop
Bay Street
☎ 246.426.5061 or 246.431.0767

Woolworth
Prince William Henry Street
☎ 246.426.5927

Sewing World
4/5 Swan Street
☎ 246.436.7902

## Bermuda

**(The country code for Bermuda is 441)**

Betty's Needle Crafts
17 Duke of York Street
St. George's
☎ 441.297.8025

Gibbons
21 Reid Street
Hamilton
☎ 441.295.0022

Needles Etc.
22 Clarence Street
St. George's
☎ no phone listed

## Cayman Islands

**(The country code for Cayman Islands is 345)**

Superstitch
Shop #39, Pasadora Place
Smith Road, George Town
(lots of fabric, little yarn)
☎ 345.949.2833

# Puerto Rico

**(Area code 787)**

**San Juan**
Madejas
410 Ave de Diego Urb Puerto Nuevo
☎ 787.781.7619

# Trinidad & Tobago

**(The country code for Trinidad and Tobago is 868)**

Craft Creators
Shop 246, Level 2
The Falls at West Mall
Westmoorings, Trinidad
☎ 868.637.6488

Naipauls Book Store and Handicraft Centre
Pro Queen Street
Arima
☎ 868.667.2569

# Central America

## Costa Rica

**(The country code for Costa Rica is 506)**

**San José**
Chic Pasamaneria
Avenida 1era calle 5y7
☎506. 2.256.5023

# Crochet Master List

The following is a list of crochet abbreviations used in patterns by yarn industry designers and publishers.

Abbreviation /Description

| | |
|---|---|
| [ ] | work instructions within brackets/as many times as directed |
| ( ) | work instructions within parentheses/as many times as directed |
| * | repeat the instructions following the single asterisk as directed |
| * * | repeat instructions between asterisks/as many times as directed or repeat from a given set of instructions |
| " | inch(es) |
| alt | alternate |
| beg. | begin/beginning |
| bet | between |
| bo | bobble |
| BP | back post |
| BPdc | back post double crochet |
| BPsc | back post single crochet |
| BPtr | back post treble crochet |
| CA | color A |
| CB | color B |
| CC | contrasting color |
| ch | chain stitch |
| ch | refers to chain or space previously made: e.g., ch.1 space |
| ch.sp | chain space |
| CL | cluster |
| cm | centimeter(s) |
| cont | continue |
| dc | double crochet |
| dc2tog | double crochet 2 stitches together |
| dec | decrease/decreases/decreasing |
| dtr | double treble |
| FL or FLO | front loop or front loop only |
| foll | follow/follows/following |
| FP | front post |
| FPdc | front post double crochet |
| FPsc | front post single crochet |
| FPtr | front post treble crochet |
| g | gram |
| hdc | half double crochet |
| inc | increase/increases/increasing |

| | |
|---|---|
| lp(s) | loops |
| m | meter(s) |
| mc | main color |
| mm | millimeter(s) |
| oz | ounce(s) |
| p | picot |
| pat(s) or patt | pattern(s) |
| pc | popcorn |
| pm | place marker |
| prev | previous |
| rem | remain/remaining |
| rep | repeat(s) |
| rnd(s) | round(s) |
| rs | right side |
| sc | single crochet |
| sc2tog | single crochet 2 stitches together |
| sk. | skip |
| sl st | slip sitich |
| sp(s) | space(s) |
| st(s) | stitch(es) |
| tch or t.ch | turning chain |
| tog | together |
| tr | treble crochet |
| trtr | triple treble crochet |
| WS | wrong side |
| yd(s) | yard(s) |
| yo | yarn over |
| yoh | yarn over hook |

# Knitting Master List

The following is a list of knitting abbreviations commonly used by yarn industry designers and publishers.

Abbreviation Description

| | |
|---|---|
| [ ] | work instructions within brackets as many times as directed |
| ( ) | work instructions within parentheses in the place directed |
| * * | repeat instructions following the asterisks as directed |
| * | repeat instructions following the single asterisk as directed |
| " | inch(es) |
| alt | alternate |
| beg | begin/beginning |
| bet | between |
| BO | bind off |
| CA | color A |
| CB | color B |
| CC | contrasting color |
| Cm | centimeter(s) |
| cn. | cable needle |
| CO | cast on |
| cont | continue |
| dec | decrease/decreases/decreasing |
| dpn | double pointed needle(s) |
| fl | front loop(s) |
| foll | follow/follows/following |
| g | gram |
| inc | increase/increases/increasing |
| k or K | knit |
| k2tog | knit 2 stitches together |
| kwise | knitwise |
| LH | left hand |
| lp(s) | loop(s) |
| m | meter(s) |
| M1 | make one—an increase—several increases can be described as "M1" |
| M1p.st | make one purl stitch |

| | |
|---|---|
| MC | main color |
| mm. | millimeter(s) |
| oz | ounce(s) |
| p or P | purl |
| pat(s) or patt | pattern(s) |
| pm | place marker |
| pop | popcorn |
| p2tog | purl 2 stitches together |
| prev | previous |
| psso | pass slipped stitch over |
| pwise | purlwise |
| rem | remain/remaining |
| rep | repeat(s) |
| rev St st. | reverse stockinette stitch |
| RH | right hand |
| rnd(s) | round(s) |
| RS | right side |
| sk | skip |
| skp | slip, knit, pass stitch over— one stitch decreased |
| sk2p | slip 1, knit 2 together, pass slip stitch over the knit 2 together; 2 stitches have been decreased |
| sl | slip |
| sl1k | slip 1 knitwise |
| sl1p | slip 1 purlwise |
| sl st | slip stitch(es) |
| ss | slip stitch (Canadian) |
| ssk | slip, slip, knit these 2 stiches together—a decrease |
| sssk | slip, slip, slip, knit 3 stitches together |
| st(s) | stitch(es) |
| St st | stockinette stitch/stocking stitch |
| tbl | through back loop |
| tog | together |
| WS | wrong side |
| Wyib | with yarn in back |
| wyif | with yarn in front |
| yd(s) | yard(s) |
| yfwd | yarn forward |
| yo | yarn over |

yrn    yarn around needle
yon    yarn over needle

# Good Stuff to Know

**Weights**
The Crafty Yarn Council's chart indicates the following:

**Lace or Cobweb :** The thinnest type available, it is only slightly thicker than thread and is best used for lace making and doilies.
Needle Size: 000.1
Hook Size: Steel 6-8 or Regular B-1

**Fingering** : Also extremely thin. It is best used for lace projects or socks.
Needle Size: 1-3
Hook Size: B1-E4

**Sport:** Very fine and perfect for using when making baby clothes or blankets. It knits up to about as thin as a simple store bought cardigan.
Needle Size: 3-5
Hook Size: E4-7

**Light Worsted:** Also known as "DK", is smooth and even-textured. It is also sometimes used for a technique called "double knitting", when you knit two strands together to create a thicker material.
Needle Size: 5-7
Hook Size: 7-I9

**Medium Worsted:** This is the "go to" for knitters and crocheters. It is used for almost anything, and is typically used for blankets and sweaters. Great too for the beginner.
Needle Size: 7-9
Hook Size: I9-K10.5

**Chunky:** Very thick and typically used for scarves and rugs. It is very bulky and can create an interesting effect. It is typically used with needle sizes in the double digits, but smaller needles and patience can create an incredibly thick and warm material.
Needle Size: 9-11
Hook Size: K10-M13

**Roving:** Unspun wool typically used for felting, but can be used with very large needles.
Needle Size: 11 and Up
Hook Size: M and Up

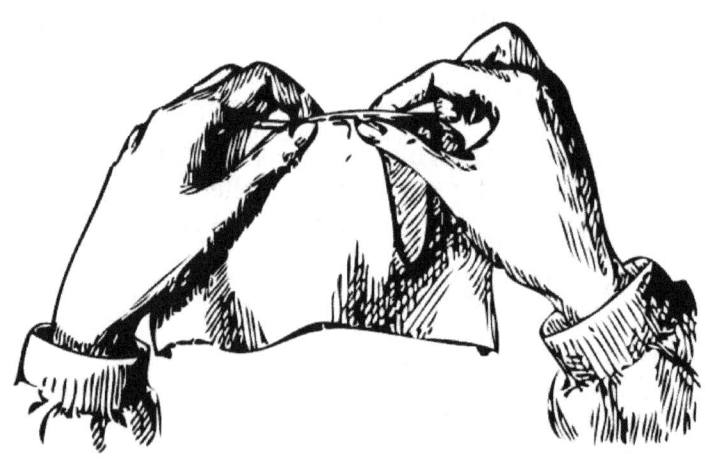

# Standard Yarn Weight System
## STANDARDS & GUIDELINES FOR CROCHET AND KNITTING
### Categories of yarn, gauge ranges, and recommended needle and hook sizes

| Yarn Weight Symbol & Category Names | 0 Lace | 1 Super Fine | 2 Fine | 3 Light | 4 Medium | 5 Bulky | 6 Super Bulky |
|---|---|---|---|---|---|---|---|
| Type of Yarns in Category | Fingering 10 count crochet thread | Sock, Fingering, Baby | Sport, Baby | DK, Light Worsted | Worsted, Afghan, Aran | Chunky, Craft, Rug | Bulky, Roving |
| Knit Gauge Range* in Stockinette Stitch to 4 inches | 33–40** sts | 27–32 sts | 23–26 sts | 21–24 sts | 16–20 sts | 12–15 sts | 6–11 sts |
| Recommended Needle in Metric Size Range | 1.5–2.25 mm | 2.25–3.25 mm | 3.25–3.75 mm | 3.75–4.5 mm | 4.5–5.5 mm | 5.5–8 mm | 8 mm and larger |
| Recommended Needle U.S. Size Range | 000 to 1 | 1 to 3 | 3 to 5 | 5 to 7 | 7 to 9 | 9 to 11 | 11 and larger |
| Crochet Gauge* Ranges in Single Crochet to 4 inch | 32–42 double crochets** | 21–32 sts | 16–20 sts | 12–17 sts | 11–14 sts | 8–11 sts | 5–9 sts |
| Recommended Hook in Metric Size Range | Steel*** 1.6–1.4mm Regular hook 2.25 mm | 2.25–3.5 mm | 3.5–4.5 mm | 4.5–5.5 mm | 5.5–6.5 mm | 6.5–9 mm | 9 mm and larger |
| Recommended Hook U.S. Size Range | Steel*** 6, 7, 8 Regular hook B-1 | B-1 to E-4 | E-4 to 7 | 7 to I-9 | I-9 to K-10½ | K-10½ to M-13 | M-13 and larger |

\* GUIDELINES ONLY: The above reflect the most commonly used gauges and needle or hook sizes for specific yarn categories.

\*\* Lace weight yarns are usually knitted or crocheted on larger needles and hooks to create lacy, openwork patterns. Accordingly, a gauge range is difficult to determine. Always follow the gauge stated in your pattern.

\*\*\* Steel crochet hooks are sized differently from regular hooks--the higher the number, the smaller the hook, which is the reverse of regular hook sizing.

This Standards & Guidelines booklet and downloadable symbol artwork are available at: YarnStandards.com

# U.S. Fiber Shows/Conventions

## January 2016

January 9-11, 2016
TNNA Winter Trade Show
San Diego Convention Center
San Diego, California

## February 2016

February 11-14, 2016
Madrona Fiber Arts Retreat
Hotel Murano
Tacoma, Washington
madronafiberarts.com

February 18-21, 2016
Stitches West
Santa Clara, California

## March 2016

March 11-12, 2016 (Fri-Sat)
Fiber Fest
Jay County Fairgrounds
4-H Building
806 E. Votaw St.
Portland, Indiana

March 11-13, 2016 (Fri-Sun)
Fiber Retreat 2016
George Washington Carver Multipurpose
Building 3804 Bald Hill Road

Jefferson City, Missouri
sites.google.com/site/fiberretreat2011/

March 18, 2016
Carolina Fiber Frolic
Sapphire, North Carolina
https://carolinafiberfrolic.wordpress.com/

March 20-25, 2016
An Island Knitting Retreat- Cat Bordhi
San Juan Island, WA

March 31, 2016
Interwearve Yarn Fest
Loveland, CO

March 31-April 3, 2016
Stitches South
Nashville, Tennessee

# April 2016

April 1-3, 2016
DFW Fiber Fest
13901 Midway Rd., Ste. 102-327
Dallas, TX 75244-4388

April 9, 2016
Stephenson County Fiber Art Fair
Jane Addams Community Center
430 W. Washington Street
Cedarville, Illinois 61013
scfaf.webs.com

April 9 - 10, 2016
Fiber Expo
Washtenaw Farm Council Grounds
5055 Ann Arbor Saline Road
Ann Arbor, Michigan 48103

April 15 -16, 2016
Yellow Rose Fiber Producers Fiesta

950 S Austin Street, County Coliseum
Seguin, TX 78155

April 21-24, 2016
PlyAway - A Spinning Retreat
Weston at Crown Center
Kansas City, Missouri
www.plyaway.com

April 30, 2016
107th Annual Sheep, Wool and Fiber Festival
Tolland Agricultural Center
Route 30, Vernon/Rockville, CT
GPS - 24 Hyde Avenue, Vernon, CT

# May 2016

May 2016- no date as of printing
Arizona – Canyon Be Chelly
☎ 970.728.6743
www.loomdancerodysseys.com

May 7-8, 2016
2016 Maryland Sheep & Wool Festival
Howard County Fairgrounds
West Friendship, Maryland
http://sheepandwool.org/2015-maryland-sheep-wool-festival-2/

May 14-15, 2016
Spring Fiber Fling
McHenry County Fairgrounds
11900 Country Club Rd.
Woodstock, Illinois
www.mchenrycountyfair.com

May 14-15, 2016
Shepherds Harvest
Lake Elmo, Minnesota
www.shepherdsharvestfestival.org

# June 2016

June 24-26, 2016
Black Sheep Gathering
Lane County Fairgrounds
Eugene, Oregon

## July 2016

July13-16, 2016
2016 TKGA CONFERENCE!
Charleston, SC

## August 2016

August 4-7, 2016
Stitches Midwest
Schaumberg, Illinois

August 17 ~ 21th, 2016
Michigan Fiber Festival
Allegan County Fairgrounds

## September 2016

September 22-25, 2016
Stitches Texas
Irving, Texas

September 24 -25, 2016
Fiber Festival
Greenwich, NY
☎ 518.692.2464

## October 2016

October 1-2, 2016
Taos Wool Festival
Taps, New Mexico

October 8, 2016
Kings County Fiber Festival
Old Stone House & Washington Park
Brooklyn, New York

October 28-30, 2016
Southeastern Animal Fiber Fair
Asheville, NC
http://saffsite.org/

# November 2016

November 6, 2016
Annual Weaving and Fiber Festival
Torrance Cultural Arts Center Adjacent
to 3341 Torrance Blvd.

November 2016- no date at this time
Yarn and Yoga
North Carolina Mountains
www.whiskeyknitters.com
☎ 404.373.1106

# International Fiber Shows/Knitting Excursions

## January 2016

**Mexico**
January 14 - 23, 2016
Oaxaca: Weaving Zapotec Dreams
**Waitlist Only**
☎ 970.728.6743 for more info

**England**
January 17, 2016
Waltham Abbey Wool Show
Essex

**England**
January 17, 2016
Wool Show
Sponsored by: The Crochet Chain &
AboutMyArea Waltham Abbey
at Marriott Hotel, Old Shire Lane,
Waltham Abbey, EN9 3LX (Junction 26 of the M25)

**Canada**
Jan. 29-31, 2016
Birch Bay Ranch
Edmonton, Alberta

# February 2016

**England**
February 19-21, 2016
Farnham Maltings
Bridge Square, Farnham
Surrey

**Guatemala**
February 28 - March 11, 2016
Guatemala's Woven Treasures
☎ 970.728.6743 for more info
www.loomdancerodysseys.com

# March 2016

**England**
March 3-6, 2016
The Spring Knitting and Stitching Show
Olympia, London

**Australia**
March 5, 2016

SpinOut
Tasmania

**New Zealand**
March 4-6, 2016
Unwind Fibrecraft Retreat
Wains Hotel
310 Princes Street
Dunedin

**Scotland**
March 17-19, 2016
Edinburgh Yarn Festival
http://www.edinyarnfest.com

**Canada**
March 18th-19th, 2016
The Eighth Annual Fibers West
Cloverdale Exhibition Park Grounds
Cloverdale, BC

# April 2016

**Holland/Belgium**
April 6-17, 2016
2016 Tour to Holland and Belgium
www.travelingtogether.net

**Scotland**
April 9, 2016
Edinburgh Workshop at Wardie

**Canada**
April 15th - 17th, 2016
Yarn Over Sleep Over
Fern Resort, Orillia, Ontario

**France**
April 19-23, 2016
Bergère de France, Reims, France
Bronagh Miskelly, featured

**Canada**
April 22-23, 2016
Creativfestival
International Centre, Mississauga
Ontario

**Peru**
April 25 - May 5, 2016
Exploring the Highlands & Machu Picchu
**Waitlist Only**
www.loomdancerodysseys.com
☎ 970.728.6743 for more info

**Argentina**
Argentina for Knitters
April 25 – May 9, 2016
www.btsadventures.com

# May 2016

**England**
May 13-14, 2016
I Knit Fandango
Royal Horticultural Halls
Lindley Hall, Elverton Street
London SW1P 2QW

**Ireland**
May 2016
Sheep's Head Yarn Festival
http://sheepsheadyarnfestival.weebly.com

# June 2016

**Canada**
June 25, 2016
Blue Hills Fibre Festival
Carberry Community Memorial Hall
Carberry, Manitoba

**Estonia**
No dates as of printing
www.loomdancerodysseys.com
☎ 970.728.6743 for more info

# July 2016

**Iceland**
July 15 – 22, 2016
Knitting in The Faroe Islands
Juliet Bernard featured
www.arenatravel.com/contact-us

**Ireland**- Loom Knitting July 2016
www.craftours.com/crafts/knitting.php

# August 2016

**Canada**
August 16, 2016
Fibrations
Fairfield Gonzales Community Place
1330 Fairfield Road
Victoria, BC
(near Moss St, beside Sir James Douglas School)

**Canada**
August 20-21, 2016
Twist
St-Andre-Avellin, Quebec, Canada
530 Rue Charles Auguste Montreuil

**New Zealand**
August 26-28, 2016
Knit August nights
Bespoke Knitters Retreat
East Pier, Ahuriri, Napier
www.knitaugustnights.co.nz

# September 2016

**Southern Africa**

September 2016- no date as of printing
Southern Africa: A Celebration of its Arts
Beads, Baskets, Tapestries and Weaving with the Elephants
www.loomdancerodysseys.com

**The Shetland Islands**
September 25 - October 2, 2016
The Shetland Islands, A Celebration of
All Things Knitting, Weaving and Sheep
☎ 970.728.6743 for more info
www.loomdancerodysseys.com

# October 2016

**Mexico**
Oaxaca: Weaving Zapotec Dreams
No date as of printing
☎ 970.728.6743 for more info
www.loomdancerodysseys.com

**Scotland**
October 3 – 18, 2016
The Highlands and Islands of Scotland
A Weaving and Knitting Adventure
www.loomdancerodysseys.com

# November 2016

**Peru**
November 3-13, 2016
Knitting Sojourn in Peru
http://catbordhi.com/workshops-events/knitting-sojourn-in-peru-with-cat-and-pecos-november-3-13-2016/

# 2017 – Plan Ahead

**New Zealand**
Knitting Tour January 2017
http://www.craftours.com/crafts/knitting.php

**Antarctica & South America**
Jan 2017
Lucy Neatby, featured
21-day cruise
www.craftcruises.com

**England**
March 1-9 2017
9 day Knitting tour
www.craftours.com/crafts/knitting.php

# Cruises

**Websites for more cruise information:**
http://www.craftcruises.com/

http://www.arenatravel.com/our-holidays/stitchtopia-knitting-crochet-holidays/view

**February 19-29, 2016**
Vogue Knitting
Southern Caribbean Seafarer
Workshop Cruise
**Holland America Line**
http://travelingtogether.net/knitting.htm

**March 31, 2016 – April 16, 2016**
China, Korea, Japan Knitting Cruise ~ Knitting
16-Day China, Korea & Japan Knitting Cruise
Gayle Roehm and Lily Chin, featured
**Holland America Line**
www.craftcruises.com

**May 2-9, 2016**
7-Day ~ Tulip Time Knitting Cruise
Ama Waterways
Chris Bylsma, featured
**Holland America Line**
www.craftcruises.com

**May 17-29, 2016**
12-Day ~ Fjords and Highlands Knitting Cruise
**Holland America Line**
www.craftcruises.com

**June 19-July 3, 2016**
14-Day ~ Baltic Knitting Cruise
**Holland America Line**
www.craftcruises.com

July 2-20, 2016
18 Day ~ Transatlantic Knitting Cruise
Maggie Jackson, featured
**Holland America Line**
www.craftcruises.com

October 7-19, 2016
12-Day ~ Canada and New England Knitting Cruise
**Holland America Line**
Ann Budd, featured
www.craftcruises.com

December 12-19, 2016
7-Day ~ Christmas Markets on the Rhine
AmaWaterways
**AmaPrima, yacht**
Chris Bylsma, featured
www.craftcruises.com

# Europe

Ahhh, welcome to beautiful Europe. What a great place to find unusual yarns that are unique in the United States. Just a few words of advice while in Europe, please please call whenever you are planning to visit one of the shops. Things are a little different if you are an American who is used to daytime retail hours. It is not uncommon for store owners to close for long vacations in the summer (3-6 weeks), siestas, or for the afternoon only to reopen in the evenings. I have included phone numbers for your convenience but please note, there are many variables to calling from city to city and country to country. Your best resource is to ask which codes are needed from the hotel or inn where you are staying. It isn't easy for us to confirm that these shops are still in business, so please call.

Culturally, in countries such as Italy for example, the sales staff prefer that you allow them to get the yarn for you. In other words, customers do not get things for themselves. So if you find a yarn of interest, please allow them to serve you!

It is also common to find yarns in places we would call a department store. If you happen to be in one, just ask and you may be pleasantly surprised at what you might find. It may be located in the basement or the back of the store.

If the store where you are shopping speaks a language other than English, I have noted the word for "yarn" just below the name of the country.

Have fun!

# Austria

(The country code for Austria is 43)
Yarn=garn

## Steiermark
Evas Bunter Garten
Grazergasse 31
Leibnitz
☎ 43.1.664 254 7096

# Belgium

(The country code for Belgium is 32)
Yarn=fil in French and garen in Dutch

## Brussels
Fil de Luxe
Chaussée de Waterloo 61
1060 Saint-Gilles
☎ 32.2.544 13 47

Kaleidoscope
Avenue Adolphe Demeur 18
☎ 32.2.544 01 30

## Etterbeek (near La Chasse)
Phildar (chain store)
Chaussee de Wavre 734
1040 Etterbeek
☎ 32. 2.649 76 75

## Ghent
Amarice
Zwijnaardsesteenweg 114
Oost.Vlaanderen
☎ 32.471.491183

## Halle
Eco-lana
Ninoofsesteenweg 50
Brabant
☎ 32.2.361 6330

## Kortrijk
Alle steken op een rij
Grote Kring 14
West Vlaanderen
☎ 32.4.774 97018

## Schaerbeek (near Diamant station)
Hollywool
Avenue des Cerisiers 22
1030 Bruxelles
☎ 32.2.733 33 75

## Sint-Michiels-Brugge
Ajour
Rijselstraat 112
West-Vlaanderen
☎ 32.050.38 9177

## Vienna
Handarbeiten Christian
Hütteldorfer Straße 157
1140 Wien
☎ 43.1.9824696

Nähzubehör + Wolle - M + M
Pribil GnbR
Währinger Str. 132, 1180
☎ 43.1.4794723

Woll-Insel
Hütteldorfer Str. 60
1150 Wien
☎ 43.1.982 88 99

Wolle und Mode
Fleischmann Ing. Eva
Neubaugasse 59/3
1070 Wien
☎ 43.1.523 33 94

**Veritas**
Nieuwstraat 123/201
1000 Brussel (located in the center of Brussels)
☎ 32.2.218 31 84

# Cyprus

(The country code for Cyprus is 357)
Yarn=νήμα

**Nicosia**
Mallia Kouvaria The Knitting Shop
35 Elia Papakyriakou Avenue
☎ 357.22.666097

# Czech Republic

(The country code for Czech Republic is 42)
Yarn= příze

**Prague**
Carolina Světlé 12
110 00 Prague 1
☎ 42.0.224.236.728

Dalin Praha s.r.o.
Rezlerova 281
109 00 Praha
☎ 42.0.274.860.304

PURL príze studio
s. armády 928/19
160 00 Prague
Praha 6, Bubenec, Dejvice
☎ 42.0.777 275 287

Shop Brno
Palacky Class
44, 612 00 Brno
☎ 42.0.541 244 627

# Denmark

(The country code for Denmark is 45)
Yarn=garn

**Bindslev**
Amimono
Ferievej 2, Tannisby 9881
☎ 45.98 93 15 93

**Copenhagen**
Anita Garn & Strik
Frederikssundsvej 171
Brønshøj, Kobenhavn
☎ 45.38.89 03 05

Rasmilla Strik & Design
Hallandsgade 3
2300 København S
☎ 45.32.97 25 75

Uldstedet
Vendersgade 3
1363 København K
☎ 45.33.91 17 7

Vandkunsten 3
1467 København K
☎ 45.33.3282 90

**Frederiksberg**
Jorun Garn
Godthåbsvej 51, 2000
☎ 45.23.30 97 67

**Fuglebjerg**
Design og Håndarbejde v/ Karen Becker
Korsoervej 4
Vestsjalland
☎ 45.55.45 48 38

# England
**(The country code for England is 44)**
**Yarn=yarn or wool**

**Bath**
Wool
19 Old Orchard Street
☎ 44.12.2546.9144

A Yarn Story
128 Walcot Street
Bath BA1 5BG
☎ 44.12.2542.9239

**Cambridge**
The Sheep Shop
72 Beche Road
CB5 8HU
☎ 44.12.2331.1268

**Cleethorpes**
A Good Yarn
53 Cambridge Street
Lincolnshire
☎ 44.14.7250.8707

**Lancashire**
& Sew What
247 Eaves Lane
Chorley
☎ 44.12.5726.7438

**London**
AbSTraCt Yarn Shop
54 Beulah Road
Walthamstow, Greater London
☎ 44.7971.255705

All the Fun of the Fair
Unit 2.8 Kingly Court
☎ 44.02.0728.72303

Bunty Wool Shop
132 Uxbridge Road
☎ 44.20.8567.8729

Fringe@Studio108
108 Alexandra Park Road
Muswell Hill
N10 2AE
☎ 44.20.8883.9478

The Good Yarn Stall
65 Brushfield S.
E1 6AA
☎ 44.75.3050.2309

The Handweavers Studio
140 Seven Sisters Road
N7 7NS
☎ 44.20.7272.1891

I Knit London
106 Lower Marsh
SE1 7AB
☎ 44.020.7261.1338

Knit with attitude
127 Stoke Newington High Street
N16 0PH
☎ 44.20.7998.3282

The London Bead Co.
Delicate Stitches
339 Kentish Town Road
NW5 2TJ
☎ 44.20.7267.9403

London Loop
15 Camden Passage
Islington
N1 8EA
☎ 44.20.7288.1160

Patricia Roberts
60 Kinnerton Street
SW1X 8ES
☎ 44.20.7235.4742

Trinity Hospice Charity Shop
85 Wilton Road
SW1V 1DN
☎ 44.20.7931.7191

The Village Haberdashery
47 Mill Lane NW6 1NB
☎ 44.20.7794.5635

Wild and Woolly
116 Lower Clapton Road
E5 0QR
☎ 44.20. 8985.5231

**Oxford**
Oxford Yarn Store
3 North Parade Avenue
OX2 6LX
☎ 44.86.560.4112

**Oxfordshire**
The Fibreworks
10 Middle Row
Chipping Norton
OX7 5NH
☎ 44.1608.645.970

# Finland

(The country code for
Finland is 358)
Yarn=lanka

**Helsinki**
Snurre
Malminrinne 1 B Helsinki
Etelä.Suomi 00180
☎ 358.040 533.5400

Tikata
Itäkatu 1.5
Etelä.Suomi 00930
☎ 358.09.7591.380

Taito Helsky
Aleksanterinkatu 26,
Etelä.Suomi 00130
☎ 358.09 6877 560

Kirstikki
Mannerheimintie 49
Etelä.Suomi 00250
☎ 358.09 2418 277

Fiina Neule
Simonkatu 12
Etelä.Suomi 00120
☎ 358.09 4 7890 065

Menita
20 Korkeavuorenkatu
Etelä.Suomi 00130
☎ 358.09 632844

# France

(The country code for
France is 33)
Yarn=Fil

**Azay le Rideau**
Mercerie Francine Ligonniere
25 rue Nationale 31790
☎ 33.02.47.45.27.66

**Bretagne**
Angora de France
Chateau de Coat-Carric
Plestin-les-Grèves
☎ 33.02.96.35.62.49

**Chinon**
Phildar
28 quai Jeanne d'Arc
37500 Chinon
☎ 33.02.47.93.42.24

**Cote d'Azur**
Caprices de Femme
20 rue Pierre Henri
Mauger 41700
☎ 33.02.54.79.53.6

Créations du Bochaine
Saint-Julien-en-Beauchene
Provence-Alpes
☎ 33.04.92.58.10.65

**Limoges**
Création Mohair
78 avenue Garibaldi
☎ 33.5.87.50.31.95

**Nice**
La Droguerie a Nice
29 rue de l'Hôtel des Postes
06000
☎ 33.4.93.04.51.47

**Paris**
Cat'Laine
19 rue St Marc
Paris, Ile-de-France
☎ 33.1.42.96.00.69

Chatmaille
2, rue Cazotte
75018
☎ 33.1.42.54.51.09

Elle Tricote Paris
7, rue Duban
☎ 33.3.88.23.03.13

La Droguerie a Paris
9 et 11 rue du Jour
75001
☎ 33.01.45.08.93.27

Lil Weasel
1 passage du grand cerf
75002
☎ 33.1.73.71.70.48

L'OisiveThé
10 rue de la Butte aux Cailles &
1 rue Jean-Marie Jégo
75013
☎ 33.1.46.27.60.86

**Plestin-les-Grèves**
Angora de France
Chateau de Coat-Carric
☎ 33.2.96.35.62.49

**Saumur**
Madame Massot
2 rue Cendrières
49400
☎ 33.2.41.51.36.54

**Toulouse**
Arrow Workshop
11, rue Sainte-Ursule
☎ 33.5.61.22.96.49

**Tours**
La Boite a Laine
67 rue du Grand
37000
☎ 33.2.47.37.76.47

**Valenciennes**
Au Fil du Temps
121 rue de Famars
Nord-Pas-de-Calais
☎ 33.3.27.41.13.90

**Vernon**
Au d'Argent
20 rue du Soleil
27200
☎ 33.2.32.51.23.85

Phildar
7 rue du Soleil
27200
☎ 33.2.32.53.43.14

**Versailles**
Phildar
23 rue Mar Foch
78000 Versailles
☎ 33.1.30.21.39.85

# Germany

**(The country code for Germany is 49)**
Yarn=Garn

## Berlin

bouclé - connect your stitches
Nassauische Strasse 11-12 10717
☎ 49.30.81.85.3014

Die WollLust
Mittenwalder Straße 49
10961
☎ 49.30.69.53.3385

Fadeninsel
Oranienstraße 23 Berlin
10999
☎ 49.30.615.6994

Frau Wolle
Bismarckstraße 76 Berlin
D.12157
☎ 49.30. 855.9181

Knit Knit
Linienstraße 154 Berlin
0115
☎ 49.309.836.6430

LaLaine
Kantstraße 145 Berlin
10623
☎ 49.30.313.8483

Loops
Wörther Straße 19 Berlin
10405
☎ 49.30.44.05.4934

Needles and Pins
Solmsstraße 31 Berlin
10961
☎ 49.30.69.81.9481

Simply Stitch - Wolle & Design
Dietzgenstraße 88
Berlin 13158
☎ 49.30.47.48.9698

Stoffhaus Berlin
Frankfurter Allee 50
Berlin 10247
☎ 49.30.291.8354

Wollrausch
Breite Straße 50
Berlin 13187
☎ 49.30.29.04.5377

## Blender, Niedersachsen

Atelier Claudia Wersing
Mühlenberg 1
☎ 49.42.33.943.0667

## Cologne

Alice-im-Wunderladen
Redwitzstraße 12
Nordrhein-Westfalen
☎ 49.17.49.90.9784

## Moenchengladbach

Atelyeah
Luetzowstraße , 41061
☎ 49.21.61.56.75267

## Munich

Die Mercerie
Nymphenburger Straße 96
80636
☎ 49.89.20.0331

Die Wolle
Müllerstraße 50
80469
☎ 49.89.26.5852

Ludwig Beck
Burgstrasse 7
80331
☎ 49.89.23.69.1402

Strickeria (unique and exotic yarns)
Georgenstraße 43,
80799
☎ 49.89.88.90.4532

Wolle Rödel
Rosental 9
80331
☎ 49.89.26.5348

**Sandhausen**
Andrea's Wollboutique
Hauptstraße 105
69207 Baden-Wurttemberg
☎ 49.62.24.2377

**Wald, Bayern**
Wollpertinger GbR
Sportplatz-Ringstrasse 14
☎ 49.09.46.33.03.9822

# Greece

(The country code for Greece is 30)
yarn= νήμα

**Athens**
Embroidery 31 LTD
Clayton 8
10560
☎ 30.21.032.22894

Kangaroocraft
Evaggelistrias 22
Athina 105 60
☎ 30.21.0323.4939

Mallia Molokotou
Kleitiou 3
Attiki
☎ 30.21.0322.4213

Mallia Sakalak
Kolokotroni 30
Attiki
☎ 30.21.0323.1710

Provataki
N.Plastira 24
15121 Marousi
☎ 30.21.5530.7493

# Hungary

(The country code for Hungary is 36)
Yarn=fonál

**Budapest**
1001fonal
Hollán Ernő utca 22
☎ 36.30.839 3518

Barka Fonal
József krt.25.
☎ 36.30. 599 1907

# Ireland

**(The country code for Ireland is 353)**
**Yarn= snáth**

**Bantry**
Bantry Yarns
New Street
County Cork
(Beside Supervalu over the Discount store)
☎ 353.8.76.186.274

**Bunmahon**
The Wool Shop
3 Osborne Terrace
County Waterford
☎ 353.51.292962

**Convoy**
Knitfield
Killynure
County Donegal
☎ 353.1.74.9147508

**Craigavon**
The Yarn Barn
19 North Street
Lurgan, Craigavon
County Armagh
BT67 9AG
☎ 44.28 3832.7923

Yarnhouse
28 Church Street
County Armagh
BT62 3LQ
☎ 44.28.3839. 3337

**Dublin**
The Constant Knitter
88 Frances Street
Dublin 8
☎ 353.1.87.996.7197

Hickeys Fabrics
Craft Store
5 Henry St, Dublin 1
☎ 353.1.873.0714

The Knitting Room
99 Malahide Road
Donnycarney
Dublin 3
☎ 353.1.87.831.4464

This is Knit
First Floor
Powerscourt Townhouse
S. William Street
Dublin 2
☎ 353.1.670.9981

**Galway**
Knitwits & Crafty Stitchers
Unit 14H
Liosban Business Park
Tuam Road
☎ 353.1.91.751.945

**Nenagh**
Black Sheep
Kickham Street
County Tipperary
☎ 353.1.87.649.3559

**Portadown**
Loughrea Needles and Wool
Barrack Street
County Galway
☎ 353.1.87.628.6179

**Thurles**
The Little Wool Shop
Old Baker Street
☎ 353.1.87.697.2512

# Northern Ireland

**(The country code for Northern Ireland is 44)**
**Yarn= snáth**

**Belfast**
Craftworld
23-29 Queen Street
☎ 44.28.9024.9000

Jeans Wool Shop
Cregagh Road
Antrim BT6 9EQ
☎ 44.28.9045.6388

# Italy

**(The country code for Italy is 39)**
**Yarn=filati**

Please call before going and ask for their hours. Many shops in Italy close in the middle of the day and reopen at 3:00pm.

**Abruzzi**
di lana e d'altre storie
Corso Umberto I 561
Montesilvano, Pescara
☎ 39.347.446.8198

**Bozen/Bolzano**
Aufburg OHG
Silbergasse 15 A
☎ 39.47.97.1506

**Florence**
Agomago
Via Arnolfo, 3/r
50121
☎ 39.55.62.66.136

Campolmi Roberto Filati
Via F. Portinari, 19/21 R
Firenze, Toscana
☎ 39.55.21.0218

Ditta Chiti, Maglieria Merceria Filati
Via di Cerchi 7/r
(in the area near Piazza della Signoria)
50054
☎ 39.55.21.2262

Filati Compolmi
Via Folco Portinari 19/21r
50122
☎ 39.55.21.5622

Filatura di Crosa
Via de' Guicciardini 21r
50125
☎ 39.55.28.9193

Fimet (S.N.C.) Filati Mercerie Tessuti
3/4/R, Piazza delle Cure
50133
☎ 39.55.57.1606

Mirko Filati Di Campi
35/R, Piazza S. Lorenzo
50123
☎ 39.55.29.4557

**Milan**
Centro Dellalana
Via Montevideo 25
20144
☎ 39.24.69.0338

Lanar
Via Nino Bixio 7
20129
☎ 39.22.94.03.050

Meazza Lane
Via Francesco De Sanctis 47
20141
☎ 39.28.95.00.931

**Montesilvano, PE**
di lana e d'altre storie
Corso Umberto I 561
☎ 39.34.74.46.8198

**Naples**
Canetta Napoli
Via Cesare Battisti 19
Campania
☎ 39.81.55.22.142

**Rome**
Branciforte
Piazza Paganica 12
Centro Storico
00186
☎ 39.06.68.65.271

Centro Lampo Roma
Via Oderisi da Gubbio 227
00146
☎ 39.06.55.78.369

Vanita di Filati
Via della Badia di Cava 88
00142
☎ 39.06.54.09.883

**Venice**
Lellabella
San Marco 3718
(Calle della Mandola)
☎ 39.41.52.25.152

# Netherlands

**(The country code for Netherlands is 31)**
Yarn=Garen

**Amsterdam**
Breiboetiek "de Vlotte Knot"
Schellingwouderdijk 251
Noord Holland 1023
☎ 31.65.534.0383

De Afstap
Oude Leliestraat 12
Noord Holland 1015
☎ 31.20.623.1445

Hand Made Heaven
Kastanjeplein 2 Amsterdam
Noord Holland 1092
☎ 31.20.638.7816

Jan - De Grote Kleinvakman
Albert Cuypstraat 203a
Noord Holland 1073
☎ 31.20.673.8247

Penelope Craft
Kerkstraat 117
Noord Holland 1017GE
☎ 31.61.427.7733

Weldraad
Haarlemmerdijk 147
Noord Holland 1013 KH
☎ 31.20.223.2800

**Joure**
Ajoure
Pastorielaan 2
☎ 31.51.341.3344

**Groningen**
Achterpand
Lage der A 1-1
9718 BJ
☎ 31.50.280. 5500

**Huissen, Gelderland**
't Hobby Hoekje
HobbyHoekje
Langestraat 29
☎ 31.26.325.3507

**Oostkapelle, Zeeland**
Atelier Bernardien
Dorpsstraat 9
☎ 31.11.858.2762

**Rotterdam**
Daisy Handwerken
Benthuizerstraat 63
Zuid-Holland
☎ 31.10.467.6254

**Uden, Noord-Brabant**
't Kluske
Galerij 17
☎ 31.41.326.3411

**Zuidlaren, Drenthe**
't Ryahuis
Telefoonstraat 26
☎ 31.50.409.2618

# Norway

**(The country code for Norway is 47)**
Yarn=garn

**Bergen**
Nilssen på bryggen
Tekstiler og -utstyrsvarer - Forretning
Bryggen 3
5003
☎ 47.55.31.67.90

Norwegian Spirit AS
Sy- og håndarbeidsartikler - Detalj
Strømgaten 4,
5015
☎ 47.94.16.63.11

**Brumunddal**
Morgrethe
Nygata 11
2380
☎ 47.62.36.61.00

**Drammen, Buskerud**
Andr. Thorkildsen Husfliden
Drammen AS
Blichsgt. 3
☎ 47.32.83.26.65

**Fredrikstad**
Alpakkahuset Gårdsbutikk
Ringstadhavna 14
☎ 47.90.17.76.32

**Oslo**
Tjorven
Valkyriegata 17
0366
☎ 47.22.69.33.60

**Molde , More og Romsdal**
Aandahls
Storgata 35
☎ 47.71.20.52.17

# Poland

(The country code for
Poland is 48)
Yarn= przędza

**Warsaw**
amiQs
Towarowa 35
☎ 48.606.20.38.20

# Portugal

(The country code for
Portugal is 35)
Yarn=bocejo

**Algés**
Tricots Brancal
R. Ernesto da Silva 22
1495
☎ 35.21.411.2043

**Laranjeiro**
Arco-íris A Metro
Alameda Guerra Junqueiro 34A
2810-072
☎ 35.21.259.6135

**Lisbon**
Adriano Coelho
Baixa
Rua da Conceição, 123
1100.153
☎ 35.21.342.6818

Casa Fontan
Estrada de Benfica, 620
1500.088
☎ 35.21.716.0461

Dotquilts
Rua dos Quarteis nº79 B
☎ 35.21.362.7173

Pra'kriar
Campo de Ourique
Praça de São João Bosco 1A
☎ 35.21.390.0481

# Russia

(The country code for
Russia is 7)
Yarn= пряжа)

**Moscow**
Moscow Spinning Factory
Malaya Semenovskaya, St. 28
☎ 7.495.748.37.99

# Scotland

**(The country code for Scotland is 44)**

**Aberdeen**
Crafty Things
Beechwood School ,Raeden Park Road
Aberdeenshire AB15 5PD
☎ 44.01.224.319.882

The Knit Hoose
36 Broad Street, Peterhead
Aberdeenshire  AB42 1BX
☎ 44.01.779.474.323

Maxwells Wools
241 Rosemount Place
Aberdeenshire AB25 2XX
☎ 44.01.224. 643.738

Tarts & Crafts
Eigie Road , Balmedie
Aberdeenshire AB23
☎ 44.01.358.742.002

Wool for Ewe
83-85 Rosemount Place
AB25 2YE
☎ 44.01.224.643.738

Dragon's Den Wools
20 High Street
Kinghorn, Fife
☎ 44.01.592.891.151

**Edinburgh**
Ginger Twist Studio
11 London Road
Midlothian
EH7 5AP
☎ 44.07.599.479.445

HK Handknit
83 Bruntsfield Place
EH10 4HG Bruntsfield
☎ 44.01.31.228.1551

Kathy's Knits
64a Broughton Street
EH1 3SA Edinburgh
☎ 44.01.315.564.837

Nifty Needles
56, High St, Linlithgow
West Lothian EH49 7AQ
☎ 44.01.506.670.435

**Glasgow**
Alice's Wool Shop
Unit 10
Huntershill Village
100 Crowhill Road
Bishopbriggs  G64 1RP
☎ 44.01.41.772.9214

CraftyJacq's
1A Common Green
☎ 44.01.357.522.227

k1 Yarns Knitting Boutique
136 Queen Margaret Drive
G20 8NY
☎ 44.01.41.576.0113

Yarn Cake
148 Queen Margaret Drive
G20 8NY
☎ 44.01.41.946.5305

# Spain

(The country code for Spain is 34)
Yarn= bostezo

**A Coruña**
Briznas
Av. Fernández Latorre, 13 – bajo
Galicia
☎ 34.881.92.3467

**Barcelona**
All You Knit Is Love
8 Carrer de la Barra de Ferro
Barcelona, 08003
☎ 34.93.310.7180

La Llana 7
Plaça De La Llana 7
Barcelona, 8003
☎ 34.93.269.1347

Llanàrium
Carrer d'Estruc, 20
Cataluña 08002
☎ 34.93.105. 6799

Llanes Travessera
Travessera de Gràcia 294
Cataluña 08025
☎ 34.03.434.5889

Merceria Santa Ana SA
Avda Portal de l'Angel 26
Barcelona, 8002
☎ 34.93.302.0948

Oyambre
Pau Claris 145
Barcelona, 08009
☎ 34.93.487.2672

**Madrid**
Black Oveja
Calle Sagasta, 7
28004 Madrid
☎ 34.91.445.326

El Punto Madrid
Calle Meléndez Valdés 68
☎ 34.91.550.0702

Lanas Alondra
Calle del Arenal, 1
28013 Madrid
Puerta del Sol
☎ 34.915.229.967

Lanas El Gato Negro
Calle de la Sal, 2
28012
☎ 34.913.665.800

Lanas Sixto
Calle Atocha 9
28012
☎ 34.915.21.7410

Marquina Labores y Complementos
Calle Eraso 10
28028, Salamanca
☎ 34.913.61.2307

**Palma de Mallorca**
Crea Corner at El Corte Inglés
Las Avenidas
(Chain store)
Avenida de Alexandre Rosello, 12
Islas Baleares
☎ 34.663.281.070

**Valencia**
Al Sol, a mano
C/ Enrique Navarro 27, bajo
☎ 34.960.017.733

# Sweden

**(The country code in Sweden is 46)**
**Yarn=Garn**

**Stockholm**
Anntorps väv
Österlånggatan 11
Stockholm 11131
☎ 46.8.67.0023

Ekens Garn
Ringvägen 64
Stockholm 11861
☎ 46.8.64.20.013

Garn & Sybehör
Sofiagatan 3
Stockholm 11640
☎ 46.8.70.20.413

Garnverket
Hantverkargatan 14
Stockholm112 21
☎ 46.8.65.17.808

Ljungqvist Garn Odenplan
Karlbergsvägen 10
Stockholm 11327
☎ 46.8.30.7020

Majas Garn och Sybehör
Katarina Bangata 49
Stockholm 11639
☎ 46.8.644.82.00

Sticka
Österlånggatan 37
Stockholm 11131
☎ 46.8.23.37.37

Trouvadi
Torkel Knutssonsgatan 29
Stockholm11640
☎ 46.8.669.85.50

Wincent Garner & Embroidery
A'faire Natur Garner
Västmannagatan 56
Stockholm 11124
☎ 46.8.34.4505

**Vittsjo**
Borgs Vävgarner AB
280 22 VITTSJÖ
Hässleholmsvägen 28
280 22
☎ 46.451.229.00

# Switzerland

**(The country code in Switzerland is 41)**
**Yarn=Garn or Filato**

**Bern**
Bastelzentrum Bern
Bubenbergplatz 11
☎ 41.31.311.06.63

Magliamania Yarns
Länggassstrasse 29
3012
☎ 41.31.301.44.02

**Colombier**
Au Fil des Saisons
Rue du Château 11
Neuchatel
☎ 41.32.841.64.64

**Geneva**
Claudine Laine Creations
Boulevard Carl. Vogt 63, Genève 1205
Tram Stop: (take trollybus 2 or 19)
☎ 41.22.321.55.74

Le Roulet
Place du Marché 5, Carouge (GE), Genève 1227
Tram Stop: Marche (Line 12)
☎ 41.22.343.4911

Manor Department Store
Rue de Cornavin 6,
Ginevra, Geneve 1201
GenevaTram Stop: (Coutance) also Cornavin train station
(Yarns are mostly in the basement)
☎ 41.22.909.46.99

The Shops/au Dé d'Argent
rue de la Servette 76, Genève, 1202
Tram Stop: Poterie (line 14)
☎ 41.22.733.06.46

Tricolaine
Rue Roi Victor Amé, Carouge (GE), Genève 1227
Tram Stop: Marche (Line 12)
☎ 41.22.301.02.42

**Zurich**
Anna Lana Handarbeiten
Rebgasse 5
8004 Zürich
☎ 41.44.241.78.18

Manor
Bahnhofstrasse 75
8001 Zürich Kreis
☎ 41.44.229.56.99

Vilfil GmbH
Kreuzstrasse 39
8008 Zurich
☎ 41.44.383 99 03

# Turkey

**(The country code for Turkey is 90)**
**Yarn =iplik**

**Izmir**
Elif Tuhafiye
Cumhuriyet Caddesi No:26/B Alacati
☎ 90.232.716.85.13

# Wales

**(The country code for Wales is 44)**
**Yarn=Edafedd**

**Aberaeron**
Rosemary's Wool Shop
Birmingham House
22 Sgwar Alban
SA46 0AH
☎ 44.545.90.5051

**Abergavenny**
Nantiago Homecrafts
49.50 Frogmore Street
Gwent NP7 5AN
☎ 44.873.85.4091

The Wool Croft
9 Cross Street
Abergavenny, Gwent
NP7 5EH
☎ 44.873.85.1551

**Ammanford**
Capricorn Wool
35 New Road
Dyfed SA18 3EY Wales
☎ 44.269.59.8405

**Bangor**
Corun I Saw dl
78 High Street , Bethesda
Gwynedd LL57 3AR
☎ 44.248.60.1780

Sew Wise
137B High Street
Gwynedd LL57 1NT
☎ 44.248.37.2246

**Beaumaris**
Pretty Things of Beaumaris
Market Square
Gwynedd  LL58 8AJ
☎ 44.248.81.0101

**Benilech**
Kit 'n Kaboodle
Banks Buildings
Anglesey LL74 8RA
☎ 44.248. 85.2111

**Betws-y-Coed**
The Welsh Wool Shop
Snowdonia National Park
North Wales LL24 OAY
☎ 44.690.71.0292

**Brecon**
Knatty Knitters
4 Market Arcade
Powys LD3 9DA
☎ 44.874.62.4088

Oyster Clothing Ltd.
28 Castle Arcade
South Glamorgan
CF10 1BW
☎ 44.292.064.4107

Shaws The Drapers Ltd.
1 Wood Street
South Glamorgan
CF10 1EL
☎ 44.292.022.8196

Wool Producers of Wales
Ffrwdgrech Road
Powys LD3 8DR
☎ 44.874.62.2754

**Carmarthen**
The Wool Baa
F2 The Market
Dyfed SA31 1QY
☎ 44.267.23.6734

**Clynderwen**
Dolau Isaf Farm
Dolau Isaf ,Mynachlogddu
Dyfed SA66 7SB
☎ 44.994.41.9327

**Dolgellau**
Knit One....
Maesgwyn, Cader Road
Gwynedd, LL40 1RB
☎ 44.341.42.2194

**Largoward**
Digilpin
16 Cupar Road,
Fife, KY9 1HX
☎ 44.334.84.0264

**Llandovery**
Cottage Workshop
6 Market Square
Dyfed SA20 0AA
☎ 44.550.72.1662

**Llandudno**
Betty's Fabrics
1 Mostyn Broadway
Gwynedd LL30 1YL
☎ 44.492.87.7282

REM Crafts
1 Zion Passage
Gwynedd LL30 2TB
☎ 44.492.87.3404

The Sewing Knitting &
Handicraft Centre
125 Mostyn Street
Gwynedd LL30 2PE
☎ 44.492.87.5269

The Windmill Wool Shop
1 Bodhyfryd Road
Conwy LL30 2DT
☎ 44.492.87.7791

**Monmouth**
B's Hive
20-22 Church Street
Gwent
☎ 44.600.71.3548

**Newport**
Hobbycraft
Harlech Retail Park
Cardiff Road
Gwent NP20 3BA
☎ 44.845.051.6540

Vince White Wholesale
47 Duckpool Road
Gwent NP19 8FL
☎ 44.633.257.733

The Wool Shack
418 Chepstow Road
Gwent NP19 8JH
☎ 44.633.279.733

**Pontyclun**
Ammonite Yarns
7 Llantrisant Road
South Wales, CF72 9DP
☎ 44.443.520.200

**Porthmadog**
Dechrau Da
17 Stryd Fawr
Gwynedd
☎ 44.766.51.4524

**Powys**
Montogomery
The Little Gallery
Broad Street
SY15 6PH
☎ 44.686.668.868

**Swansea**
H R Jones & Co.
68 High Street ,Clydach
West Glamorgan SA6 5LN
☎ 44.792.842.202

Knitters and Sewers World
21.22 Park Street
West Glamorgan SA1 3DJ
☎ 44.792.456.444

Mrs. Mac's
2 Woodville Road ,Mumbles
West Glamorgan SA3 4AD
☎ 44.792.369.820

Ystradgynlais Wool Shop
1 Station Road ,Ystradgynlais
West Glamorgan SA9 1NT
☎ 44.639.843.565

**Tenby**
Fibre Factory
1 White Lion Street
Pembrokeshire SA70 7ES
☎ 44.834.845.951

Wrexham
RKM Wools
Stalls 7, 15 & 20 ,The Peoples Market
Wrexham LL13 8BY
☎ 44.978.266.774

# South America

Finding shops in South America has been challenging to say the least, but not because there are none. Rather, they are not easily researchable through the internet, which means I have had to rely on blogs and others' travel information. Although my list is limited, it in no way represents the many vendors along the roads in Peru, or the co-ops or other locations where you may find yarns. Often, cities will have blocks of stores that have yarns for sale in addition to other wares; so for that reason, you will find references to streets or blocks. On a final note, I was surprised to read that although Peru is notorious for its alpaca, most often it is exported to other countries (such as the U.S.) in order to be spun into yarn that we purchase in our local American yarn shops.

Helpful words while traveling in South America:

| English | Spanish |
| --- | --- |
| yarn | hilo |
| gauge | muestra del punto |
| swatch | muestra |
| cast on | montar |
| bind off | cerrar |
| knit stitch | punto derecho |
| purl stitch | punto revés |
| knitting/to knit | labor de punto/hacer punto |
| knitting needles | agujas de punto |
| yarn store | laneria |
| cashmere | cachemira |
| acrylic | acrílico |
| wool | lana |
| silk | seda |
| alpaca | alpaca |

# Argentina

(The country code for Argentina is 54)
Yarn=hilo

**Buenos Aires**
Arte Natural
Scalabrini Ortiz 1019
Buenos Aires, Argentina
☎ 54.9.11 4530.3223

Milana Hilados
Av. Raúl Scalabrini Ortiz 1062
C1414DNX CABA
☎ 54.9.11 4777.1346

Yanabey
Av Raul Scalabrini Ortiz
925, 1414 Ciudad Autonoma
☎ 54.810.444.9262

Many of the shops in Buenos Aires are on Avenida Scalabrini Ortiz just southwest of Avenida Cordoba, toward Avenida Correintes. The Malabia metro station is on the corner of Correintes and Scalabrini Ortiz, which is 1 km away from the corner of Cordoba and Corrientes. Within a half of a kilometer from that intersection, you should see your first yarn shop.

# Brazil

(The country code for Brazil is 55)
Yarn =fio

**Rio Grande do Sul**
Ecolã
Av. Pereira Passos, 1152
Porto Alegre,
☎ 55.51.3268.0123

Fazenda Caixa Dágua
Dilermando de Aguiar - RS
Rio Grande do Sul
☎ 55.11.3612-4265

**São Paulo**
Empório das Lãs
Rua Conde de Porto Alegre
1711 - Campo Belo
☎ 55.11.5531.3086

Novelaria
R. Mourato Coelho
678 – Pinheiros
05417-011
☎ 55.11.3729.7188

Pintar E Bordar
Loja de artigos para tricô
Alameda dos Jurupis
1276 - Indianópolis,
04088-004
☎ 55.11.5561.2261

# Chile

**(The country code for Chile is 56)**
Yarn=hilo

**La Ligua**
De Origen Chile
Portales 243
☎ 56.33.271.6889

**Puerto Montt**
Lanas para ti
Urmeneta 580
local 229 Mall Paseo Del Mar
☎ 56.6.528.2066

**Santiago**
Santiago, as it turns out, has its own yarn district. The main street is called **21 de Mayo**. There you will find lots of yarn shops for you to peruse. How to get there: take the metro to the Cal and Canto station on the yellow line and exit on Puente street. Go straight off the escalator and the second street that you come across will be Rosas street- go left on Rosas. Rosas dead ends on 21 de Mayo street, and you will find an entire street block of "lanerias" (yarn shops). I have one listed below, although there are so many more! Note: yarns are behind the counter and often the yardage is not on the skein, so you will have to enlist the help of the shop owner.

Lanas e Hilos Lanas Dina
21 de Mayo 657
RM Santiago
☎ 56.2.2632.8371

# Colombia

**(The country code for Colombia is 57)**

**Bogata**
Tienda de Hilos
Cra. 98a #61B-16 sur
☎ no phone listed

Casa Rosada
Calle 64, 0-4-94
Santa fe de Bogota
☎ 57.1.2493063

Hilo Todo Color
30, Carrera 13 #13
☎ 57.1.282.2322

# Peru

**(The country code for Peru is 51)**
**Yarn=hilo**

Although I have never traveled to Peru, they say that for an alpaca yarn addict, you struck gold! In Arequipa for example, my research shows that you will find locals selling their yarn and goods in public markets and along the roadside. The colors you will find are astounding. I have also learned that there are many shops in Arequipa that are small but carry a decent selection of yarn.

**Arequipa**
Michell & Cia
Juan de la Torre 101
San Lázaro Arequipa
☎ 51.54 202525

**Cusco**
Michell & Cia
Calle Granada 291
Cercado Cusco
☎ 51.84. 601434

**Lima**
El Paraiso de las Lanas
Calle Lima No 629 - Int. 1
(CC.Gamarrita) - Nasca
☎ no phone listed

**Miraflores**
MICHELL Alpaca Yarn Store
Av. Benavides 1730
☎ 51.01.6512327
(on the corner of Av. Alfredo Benavides and 25 De Mayo between a Billabong store and a Scotabank)

# Uruguay

**Yarn=lana**
**(The country code for Uruguay is 598)**

**Montevideo**
Manos del Uruguay Yarns Outlet
San Jose 1111 CP: 11100
☎ 598.2900 4910

# Africa

Africa, a place where we think of safaris and wild animals, not particularly knitting. As with many countries in Africa and Asia, you will find that it is unusual to find a stand alone, brick and mortar yarn store. Instead you may see a tiny shop that sells kitchen goods, clothing, fabric, shoes and maybe some acrylic yarn. For that reason, it is so difficult to find more shops like the ones listed. If you are going to Africa for a visit, you may want to bring some yarn from home (excluding S. Africa), but also step into one of these shops, you may be pleasantly surprised!

# Egypt

(The country code for Egypt is 20 )
Yarn= ghazal

**Alexandria**
Cristal
8 El Tahreer Square
Al Mansheya
☎ 20.480.9375

# Kenya

(The country code for Kenya is 254)
Yarn= uzi

**Nairobi**
The Woman Shop
1st floor, Sarit Center
Westland
☎ 254.020.374.8374

Spinner's Web
Getathuru Gardens, off Peponi Road
Spring Valley
☎ 254.020.207.2629

# South Africa

(The country code for South Africa is 27)
Yarn= nokotini, yarn

**Pretoria**
94 Anderson Street
(corner of Anderson & William streets next to Doxa Deo)
Brooklyn, Pretoria
☎ 27.012.362.8689

Wolmart
85 Retief Street
☎ 27.012.327.7662

**Western Cape**
The Wool Studio
25 Market Street
George
☎ 27.44.873.5382

A B C Knitting and
Haberdashery Centre
Colin Wade St & Haley Avenue,
Parkhill Gardens
Germiston, Gauteng
☎ 27.011.827.4296

# Asia

What an exciting place to be - Asia! The smell of spices, the car horns that blow much more than anyone can ever imagine and the taste of food that is so fragrant, that you might even dream about it. And of course, the yarns. Yarns vary in Asia, from the acrylics to the yaks. There is a huge spectrum of yarn here but most of the time, it won't be showcased in yarn shops, for which the modern world is so accustomed. Instead, you will have to do some searching in stores that may also sell house wares, clothing, shoes, bicycles, etc. Nonetheless, I have managed to list the shops that I have found for your convenience. I always recommend calling if possible and if you don't speak the local language, have someone call for you to confirm the address and working hours. Traveling within some of these countries is tedious, so always allow extra time. Now go buy some yarn!

## Bahrain

**(The country code for Bahrain is 973)**
**Yarn= ghazal**

Things-to-do
Located along Budaiya Highway near the flyover
Shop 609, Building 611, Road 2621
Jidd Hafs
☎ 973.1.759.0409

## Bhutan

**(The country code for Bhutan is 975 )**
**Yarn=yarn**

Historically, almost all weavers in Bhutan made their own yarn and dyed it with natural pigments. Chemically dyed yarns in a broad palette were introduced to Bhutan in the early twentieth century, but today there is a resurgence of interest in and demand for textiles woven from naturally dyed, homespun yarns. If you are a weaver, you hit the jackpot in Bhutan!

There is a yarn shop in **Trasigang**, with additional yarns from India. It is primitive and the store front unmarked, but ask around and you should be able to find it!

# Brunei

(The country code for Brunei is 673)
Yarn= benang

**Bandar Seri Begawan**
Nyneish Books, Arts and Crafts
Unit B6, Ground Floor
Crowne Princess Complex
☎ 673.224.0994

The best way I can think of to describe its location is that it is behind the Charcoal Restaurant in Seri. Either drive around or walk-through Charcoal. You won't miss it.

# Cambodia

(The country code for Cambodia is 855)
Yarn= ambaoh

Knitting and crocheting are not hugely popular in Cambodia, but there are some supplies available at local markets. In addition to the shops listed below, Ou Ruessei market (not touristy) located in central Phnom Penh has some yarn, buttons, scissors, hoops, embroidery threads and of course, needles and hooks. Hint: The craft supply shops are mostly on the top floor.

**Phnom Penh**
Ou Ruessei Market
☎ 855.12.403.940i 1

Tuol Tom Poung Market
(also known as the Russian Market)
155, Phnom Penh
☎ no phone listed

Cambodian Creations
House 116, Street 113
Phnom Penh 12304
☎ 855.23.631.7914

# China

**(The country code for China is 86 )**
**yarn=** 纱**Shā**

Helpful words while travelling in China:

| | |
|---|---|
| knitting | 针织Zhēnzhī |
| crocheting | 钩针Gōuzhēn |
| cotton | 棉 (mian2), 棉花 ( mian2 hua) |
| linen | 亚麻 (ya4 ma2) |
| alpaca wool | 驼 羊 毛 (tuo2 yang2 mao2) |
| cashmere | 羊 绒 (yang2 rong2), 开士米 (kai1 shi4 mi3) |
| silk | 丝 (si1), 真丝 (zhen1 si1) |
| bamboo yarn | 竹纤 (zhu2 xian1), 竹纤维 (zhu2 xian1 wei2) |
| nylon | 尼龙 (ni2 long2) |
| lambswool | 小羊毛 ( xiao3 yang2 mao2) |
| Acrylic | 腈纶 |
| mercerized | 丝光防缩 |
| Bulky Acrylic | 膨体腈纶 |
| Viscose | 粘胶 |
| Tencel | 天丝 |
| Merino Wool Yarns | 美丽(利)奴(诺)羊毛纱 |

## Beijing: Qing He Mao Fang Cheng

**Wool City:** Many shops are found here, so keep your eyes open for yarn, even though it may be tucked away in the back of the store!

Directions to Wool City: Take Badaling Expressway and get off at exit 6 (Qing He). 'Wool Spinning City' building. There is a McDonalds at the bottom of this 5 floor building.
清河毛纺城
地址：八达岭高速，小营出口出来，一直往北，路右手边有个牌子。在第一个红绿灯左转，开到麦当劳的楼（毛纺城就在这个楼里）。

### Hint: Try Shop # 321
☎ 86.010.6294.5446

## Beijing: Dong Cheng District
Wan Sha Jin Dian
Wansha Wool/Cashmere Store 万纱经典纺织品
Selling a wide range of local yarns, buttons and needles, this shop is very close to Wangfujing.
No 14-2 Deng Shi Kou Da Jie
灯市口大街１４-２
Ground floor

Dong Cheng District
万纱经典纺织品
北京市东城区灯市口大街１４-２号
☎号 86.010.6512.7090

96 Dong Zhi Men Nei da Jie
Dong Cheng District
东城区东直门内大街196
☎号 86.010.6407.1770

120 Xiao Dao Kou Nan Da Jie. Dong-Cheng District 东城区交道口南大街120
☎号86.010. 8404.8415

## Beijing: Chongwen District
Yizhao Yarn Store
Liang Guang Lu, ChongWen District.
Directions: 亿兆商店．崇文区两广路边上的光明日报社的西南角了！可能你还不明白，就是：
1.
台基厂往南走祈年大街，过两广路后再往南，路西就到了！    2.
从崇文门上两广路，往西走，到光明日报社的十字路口，左转，路西就到了!
有个小店上写着"毛线和羊绒"的地方就是。
☎ 86.010.6707.5620/21

1 Guang Qu Men Wai Ma Chuan. ChongWen District
崇文区广渠门外马圈1
☎号 86.010.6778.0542

45A An Le Lin Lu, ChongWen District
崇文区安乐林路甲45
☎号 86.010.8726.7522

## Beijing: Xuan Wu District
Daqian Yarn Stores
(This is a chain and has a few locations)
Xuan Wu District.
96A, Yong An Lu
Xuan Wu District
宣武区永安路甲96
☎号 86.010.6303.8504

## Beijing: Xi Cheng District
6 Xin Jie Kou Wai Da Jie
Xi Cheng District
西城区新街口外大街6
☎号 86.010.6202.0352

## Shanghai
Shokay Yarn
This yarn is sold in at least six locations in Shanghai. There are too many stores to list here, so I can suggest that you search their website for more addresses: www.shokay.com
Shokay sells only 100% Yak and yak blended yarn. Below is one listed in Shanghai:

Shanghai Super Brand Mall (正大广场)
2F03, 168th, West Lujiazui Road (near Lujiazui Huan Road)
Lujiazui, Pudong New Area, Shanghai Road
168 2F03 (near Lujiazui Ring)
☎ 86.21.6445.8023

## Mongolia
Daquian Yarn Store
Daban Street Bairin Youqi
Chifeng, Inner Mongolia
☎ no number listed

## YinZhou District
The YinTai（宁波鄞州万达银泰百货店）
The YinTai (Ningbo Wanda Intime Department Store)
3F, # 999 Middle Siming Road, , Ningbo, Zhejiang
Siming Road 999, 3rd Floor
Wanda Intime Ningbo Yinzhou District
☎ no number listed

# Estonia

**(The country code for Estonia is 372)**
**Yarn=lõng**

## Tallinna Lõngapoed
Tallinna Kaubamaja
B korpuse galerii, I korrus
Avatud E-P 9-21
Gonsiori 2, Tallinn 10143
☎ 372.6601.763

Kadaka lõngapood
Avatud E-R 10-20 / L 10-18 / P 11-16
Kadaka tee 56C, Tallinn
☎ 372.656.7733

**Tartu Lõngapood**
Tartu Kaubamaja
3. korrus
Avatud E-L 9-21, P 10-19
Riia 1, Tartu 51004
☎ 372.7343.280

# Hong Kong

(The country code for Hong Kong is 852)
Yarn=yarn

Cheer Wool Co.
1G/F Tai Sang Commercial Building
24-34 Hennessy Road
Wan Chai
☎ 852.2527.3901

Double Knit Yarn & Co.
1/F 179-181 Fa Yuen Street
Mong Kok
Kowloon
☎ 852.2.396.2070

Elegant Company
23-25 Pilkem Street
Yau Ma Tei, Kowloon
☎ 852.2.730.0013

**Filo Kilo** G/F 167 Sai Yee Street
Mongkok, Kowloon
☎ 852.2.392.9729

# India

(The country code for India is 91)
Yarn in Hindi= Dhāgā

**Bangalore**
Bombay Embroidery Stores
14 Raja Market, Avenue Road
Bangalore – 560 002
☎ 91.80.2223.7311

Prakash Fancy Store
58, Raja Market Avenue Road
☎ no phone listed

Ramdev Fancy Store
Nagraj Complex, Raja Market
Avenue Road
☎ no phone listed

Surya Emporium
325 Narayana Pillai Street
(Off Commercial Street)
☎ 91.80.2558.9890

Our Own Store (Eastern)
327 Narayana Pillai Street
(Off Commercial Street)
☎ 91.80.2558.7785

Ravi's Craft Shop – Kalyan Complex
2nd Cross Commercial Street
☎ 91.80.2558.9780

Prakash Fancy and Gift Centre
302/2, Kaggadasapura Main Road
C.V. Raman Nagar
Bangalore –560093
☎ 91.80.2534.7285

## Bombay/Mumbai
Pradhan Stores
125/127 Bazar Gate Street
Perin Nariman Street, Fort G.P.O.
(Behind Bora Bazar)
Mumbai 400001
☎ 91.022.6635.6115

Hasmukhlal Shantilal & Co
Gandhi International
102/9, Banian Street,
Jain Mansion 1st Floor
Opp. 3rd Bhoiwada,
Pydhoni, Mumbai 400003

This is near Sena Bhavan. If you walk towards Mahim from Sena Bhavan on the Main Road, it is on the the left side a little after Camlin Studio past Raja Rani Travels. He sometimes has good collection of variety of yarn.

## Chandigarh
Jain Wool House
Sec.29.C, Shop no.48
Palika Bazar
☎ 91.98.8847.6345

Fancy Wool House
Sec.9 SCF.48
Panchkula
☎ 91.98.1548.2377

## Chennai
Raja Thread Store
R S Shopping Centre
No.73, LB Road, Adyar
Chennai.20
☎ 91.2445.3193/39123193

Kareem's
Convent Junction, Ernakulam
☎ 91.0484 2354288/5520999

## Coimbatore
Bombay Novelty Stores
Old no.387, New no.148
Ganesh Building, D.B. Road
R.S.Puram
Tamil Nadu 641002
☎ 91.422.436.9226

## Darjeeling
M/S Wool Emporium
Knitting Wool & hosiery Merchants
N B Singh Road
Darjeeling 734101
☎ 91.0354.225.3102

## Hoshiyarpur
Ludhiyana Oswal house
☎ 91.0188.222.0873
☎ 91.92.1750.0022

Pahwa Wool Stores
Bassi Khawaju, Hoshiarpur
Punjab 146001
☎ 91.0188.222.7509

## Hyderabad & Secunderabad
BS Kamaladevi & Sons
4.3.747 Sultan Bazar
Hyderabad, Telegana 500095
☎ 91.40.2475.4468

Sheeba Corner
2.1.188/B Mahatma Ghandi Road
General Bazaar
Secunderabad 500003 AP
☎ 91.40.2781.3392

**Jabalpur**
Subhash General Stores
62, Sadar Main Road
opp Cantt Post Office
Sadar, Jabalpur
☎ 91.076.126.23081

**Kolkata**
Guin Wool House
"Jasoda Bhavan"
167/c Rash Behari Avenue
Kolkata 700 019
It is located near the junction of Gariahat Rd & Rash Behari Rd.
☎ 91.79.4005.8925

**New Delhi**
A K Woollen Industries
1267/1 first floor, Nala Road,
Sadar Bazar
New Delhi 110006
☎ 91.98.11.3296.4607

Bala Ji Wool Center
I-36A Central Market
Lajpat Nagar II
New Delhi
☎ 91.98.107.20272

Kamal Cloth House,
125 Khanna Market
Lodhi Colony
☎ 91.98.246.91872

New Kalpana Tracers
Shop No. 120 (Opposite Vegetable market),
Sarojini Nagar Market
☎ 91.98.2410.1702/2467.8396

Punjab Woollen Co
L.92 Main Road
D.D.A. Munirka,
Delhi 110067
☎ 91.98.11.2610.0164

Woolworth
32, Central Market
Ashok Vihar
New Delhi
☎ 91.98.11.2742.9358

**Pune**
Samrat Woollen House
23, Bhau Maharaj Lane
Shukrawar Peth
Near Mandai 411002
☎ 91.20.2445.1260

**Himachal Pradesh**
BD & Sons
Bhoot Nath Bazaar
Mandi 175001 (HP)
☎ 91.94.184.98086

# Indonesia

(The country code for Indonesia is 62)
Yarn= benang

**Jakarta**
Shavella
Season City Mall, LG C1#1
☎ 62.813.1854.1551

Miki Moko
Plaza Blok M
Jl. Bulungan No. 76
Kebayoran Baru
Jakarta Selatan, 12130
☎ 62.21.7590.6257

# Israel

**(The country code for Israel is 972)**
Yarn= choot חוט
Yarn= ghazal

Helpful words while travelling in Israel:

| | |
|---|---|
| Yarnshop | Cha.NOOT TZE.mer |
| Knitting | Sri.GAH |
| Wool | TZE.mer צמר |
| Cotton | Koot.NAH כותנה |
| knitting needles | Mas.ray.GOAT |
| crochet hook | Mas.RAY.gah Eh.CHAT |
| knitting pattern | Dug.MAH Le.Sri.GAH |

## Haifa and the North

**Kiryat Motzkin**
Chutshelchen
57 Goshen Blvd.
☎ 972.04.870.8309

Tzemer Esti
29 Trumpeldor
☎ 972.04.823.1370

Wool Centre
107 Jaffa
☎ 972.04.852.3102

Dahlia Wool
2 Pioneer Hadar
☎ 972.86.235.9324

Victoria Wool
60 Pioneer
☎ 972.04.862.3028

Estee wool
Trumpeldor 29
Neve Shaanan
☎ 972.04.823.1370

Junction buttons
Square Meyer Hope 4,
K. Eliezer
☎ 972.04.852.0189

## Tel Aviv and the Sharon

**Tel Aviv**
Ha'Tachana
101 Dizengoff St.
☎ 972.03.527.8825

Tzemer Pninah
25 Menashe Ben Israel
☎ 972.03.688.0661

Marietta
53 Arlozorov Street
☎ 972.03.523.5445

**Ramat Gan**
Yehudit Du'ab
14 Haro'eh
☎ 972.03.643.4007

**Givataim**
Wooly 18
Sirkin
☎ 972.03.672.5677

Kolbo Tec
31 Katznelson
☎ 972.03.731.0940

**Bnei Brak**
Hoot v'Echut
28 Nehamiah
☎ 972.03.618.0358

**Bat Yam**
Caftorei Shik
90 Balfour Street
☎ 972.03.659.2989

**Kfar Saba**
Beit Hasidkit
2 Sokolov Street
☎ 972.09.748.2381

Sidkit Inbal
94 Weitzman Street
☎ 972.09.765.8063

**Ra'anana**
Sarah Cohn
81 Ahuza Street
☎ no phone listed

**Ra'annana**
The Gourmet Yarn Shop
111 Ahuza St.
☎ 972.09.742.7020

# Jerusalem and the Shomron

**Jerusalem**
Bet HaTzemer
234 Yaffo
☎ 972.02.538.0206

Shani Badim
34 Ben Yehuda
(City Cellar)
☎ 972.02.624.1597

Themrei Rachel Cohen
Beit va.Gan 61
☎ 972.02.420. 397

Pashosh
23 Hillel Street
☎ 972.02.625.5961

# Japan

**(The country code for Japan is 81)**
**Yarn=ito**

### Japanese Lace
Japanese patterns very often combine lace, cables, bobbles, and other unusual types of stitches. The results are, at the same time, elaborate and elegant. Each level of the garment may include simpler motifs and stitches used in other portions to build on one another. A ribbing may include a simple bobble that is used together with cables on the collar of a sweater, and further combined with lace for the main body or the sleeves. The Japanese also use all different kinds of decreases. I think the Japanese knitting charts are by far the clearest charts used today. My favorite thing is that there is a Japanese national standard for knitting charts, so their symbols are the same in every book published in Japan!

### Kobe-shi
Doi Shugei
Sannomiya Center Ichigai,
Sannomiya-cho
1-5-22 Chuo-ku
Kobe, Hyogo
☎ 81.078.331.1573

### Kyoto
Avril
SACRA building 3F, 20 Nakano-cho,
Tominokoji Nishi-iru, Sanjo-dori, Nakagyo-ku
604-8083
☎ 81.075.211.2446

Habu Textiles Kyoto
Okuyama Building, 2F
Oike-sagaru, Gokomachi
Nakagyo-ku, Kyoto 604-8095
☎ 81.075.754.8200

### Tokyo
Classe
Daikanyama –Yubinbango150-0034
Shibuya-ku
Tokyo Daikanyamacho 18-3
Nakano building 1F
☎ 81.036.277.5039

Hitsujidama
BLDG1F
Fuchu Shinmachi 1-66-16
Fukui BLDG 1F
☎ 81.080.3174.5421

Moorit
Kitte 4F, 2-7-2
Marunouchi, Chiyoda-ku
☎ 81.03.6256.0843

# Kuwait

**(The country code for Japan is 81)**
**Yarn= ghazal**

Needle and thread for fabrics
Kuwait
Hawalli Ibn Khaldun Badawi Tower
Street shop # 7 in front of Osman complex
☎ 81.6.9999.666

Salmiya
Barak Trading Company
Mabroor Complex, Hamed Al Mubarak Street
☎ 81.965 2574 6727/ 8

Crafty
Kaifan Mall-basement
☎ 81.249.15965

# Lebanon

**(The country code for Lebanon is 961)**
**Yarn=ghazal**

**Beirut**
y.knot
Saifi Village
Mkhalissiya street 162
☎ 961.1.992211/961.70.108608

# Malaysia

**(The country code for Malaysia is 60)**
**Yarn = benang**

**Pulau Pinang**
Cotton House Store
No. 99A, Lorong 1/SS2
Bandar Tasek Mutiara
Simpang Ampat
☎ 60.2.730.0013

**Petaling Jaya**
Mayfair Handicraft
F19A 1st Floor Jalan 1 / 21
46460
☎ 60.3.778.52318

# Nepal

**Yarn= Yārna यार्न**

I would be terribly remiss if I didn't recognize Nepal for its beautiful wool, yak and recycled Sari yarns. Nepal's yarns are remarkably vibrant and beautiful but unfortunately, I cannot find any shops with addresses. I can only say that once you get to Nepal, you will be surrounded by yarn and co-ops of women who are knitting for a source of income. Take it all in because Nepal has yarns that aren't easily found anywhere else in the world.

# Pakistan

(The country code for Pakistan is 92)
Yarn= ਧਾਗੇ Dhāgē

**Islamabad**
The Wool Shop
G.9 Markaz
☎ 92.346.505.7858

**Lahore**
United Wool House and Garments
Chwak Darbi Bazar, rangMahal
☎ 92.042.765.6613

Singhar house
Neela Gumbad and Iqbal town
Lahore, Pakistan
☎ 92.42.3731.0164

There are also many yarn shops in Ichra Bazar, Feroze Pur Road Lahore.

# Philippines

(The country code for Philippines is 63)
Yarn= humikab

**Manila**
Dreams Yarnshoppe
3rd Floor, Glorietta 5
Ayala Center
Makati
☎ 63.2.856.0741

# Qatar

(The country code for Qatar is 974)
Yarn = ghazal

Today's Fashion
Airport Road (next to Qatar Airways)
Doha, Qatar
☎ no phone number listed

Al Rawnaq Trading Center
Shopping Mall
Jabr Bin Mohd Street
Doha, Qatar
☎ no phone number listed

Singer Fredonia Store
Al Muthaf Street (call for directions)
Doha, Qatar
☎ 974.4443.5731

# Saudi Arabia

(The country code for Saudi Arabia is 966)
Yarn= ghazal

**Al-Khobar**
Al-Zamil Stores
Prince Turkey Street
Al Khobar Al Shamalia 34429
☎ 966.13.864.1919

Al Zamil Stores
Al-Khobar 31952
☎ 966.03.898. 3232

# Singapore

(The country code for Singapore is 65)
Yarn=yarn

Wish I were Stitching
The Commerze@1 Irving Place
#01-03, Singapore 369546
☎ 65.9657.0204

Golden Dragon
(near China Town)
101 People's Park Centre
Upper Cross Street #02-51
Singapore 058357
☎ 65.6535. 8454

Spotlight Singapore
Level 5, 68 Orchard Road
(Located at the Dhoby Ghaut MRT),
Singapore, SG 0000
☎ 65. 6733.9808

Elsie Departmental Store
Blk 709 Ang Mo Kio Ave 8 #01-2607
Singapore 560709
☎ 65.6452.3366

Ishida Craft Center
163 Tanglin Road #01-04
TANGLIN MALL
Singapore 247933
☎ 65.6737.3342

Siew Lip
No 1 Jurong West Central 2 #03-01
Jurong Point Shopping Centre
Singapore 648886
☎ 65.6861.0020

Ebest Collection
587 Bukit Timah Road
#02-18 Coronation Plaza
Singapore 269424
☎ 65.6453.2628

Yon Hearn
2-12 Holland Village
211 Holland Road
☎ 65.6468.3659

# South Korea

(The country code for South Korea is 82)
Yarn= yan 얀

**Seoul**
Dongdaemun Market
Enormous shopping stadium- closes at 6pm, so get there in plenty of time. Most of the yarn shops are on the basement level.

# Taiwan

(The country code for Taiwan is 886)
Yarn=纱 Shā

## Taipei City
Shilin Yarn Supermarket
(士林毛線超市)
2F, 607, Zhongshan N. Road Sec 5, Taipei City
(台北市中山北路五段607號2樓)
☎ 886.02.2831.3777

Bear Mama (小熊媽媽)
51, Yanping N Road Sec 1, Taipei City
(台北市延平北路一段51號)
☎ 886.02.2550.8899

Luxury fibers
Knitting Trend (時尚手編)
228, Changan E Road Sec 2, Taipei City
(台北市長安東路二段228號)
☎ 886.02.2777.2930

Lin Lin (Lin Lin毛線屋)
5-9, Lishui Street Taipei City
(台北市麗水街5-9號)
☎ 886.02.2392.4289

# Thailand

(The country code for Thailand is 66)
Yarn= Sênd̂āy เส้นด้าย

## Bangkok
Siam Paragon Department Store
991/1, Rama I Road
Bangkok 10330
☎ 66.2.610.8000

Central Chidlom Department Store
1027 Thanon Phloen Chit Lumphini
Pathum Wan, Bangkok 10330, Thailand
☎ 66.2.793.7777

Knit'n Us
57/152 อาคาร Silom Terrace
ซอย ศาลาแดง 2 ถนน คอนแวนต์ Silom, Bang Rak
Bangkok 10500
☎ 66.2.635.5090

## Chiang Mai
Pinn Shop
Sewing Shop
Central Plaza Chiangmai Airport
2, Central Plaza Chiang Mai Airport 3rd Floor, Mahidol Road, Tambon Haiya Amphoe Maung Chiang Mai, 50100, 50200,
☎ 66.53.271.699

**Sukhumvit**
Bigknit Cafe
88  The Natural Park Building
(next to Dental Hostital)
Sukhumvit 49
☎ 66.2.260.5050

# United Arab Emirates

**(The country code for the UAE is 971)**
**Yarn= ghazal**

**Abu Dhabi**
Green Branch Establishment
Readymade Garments
Zayed 1st Street (Electra Road)
☎ 971.2.621.4507

**Dubai**
Craft Land Retail Store
First Floor, Town Centre Jumeirah
Jumeira Beach Road
☎ 971.4.342.2237

Creative Minds
Al Barsha
Umm Suqeim Road
Al Barsha 2
☎ 971.4.323.7180 / 4.323.7181

Creative Minds
Jumeirah
Beach Center, Beach Road
Ground Floor, Shop No. 17 & 22
☎ 971.4.344.6628

# Vietnam

**(The country code for Vietnam is 84)**
**Yarn = sợi**

**Saigon**
Kem Nghia's Shop
162 Le Thanh Ton Street
☎ no phone number listed

# Australia

**(The country code for Australia is 61)**
**Yarn=yarn**

## New South Wales

Banksia Yarns
Shop 7 Magnolia Mall
285 Windsor Street
Richmond NSW 2753
☎ 61.040.127.9853

Black Sheep Wool 'n' Wares
118 Bradley Street
Guyra NSW 2365
☎ 61.2.6779.1196

## Queensland

Yarn Over
Shop 1, 265 Blaker Road
Keperra
Brisbane
☎ 61.7.3851.2608

## South Australia

Barb's Sew and Knits
2 Byron Street
Glenelg, SA 5022
☎ 61.8.8294.7441

Bennett and Gregor
24 Seventh Street
Gawler South Australia 5118
☎ 61.8.8522.2169

Country Chix
17 Graves Street
Kadina SA 5554
☎ 61.8.8821.2800

Craft Alley Designs
8 Main Road McLaren Flat
Adelaide, SA 5171
☎ 61.407.826.478

## Tasmania

The Stash Cupboard
159 Liverpool Street
Hobart, TAS 7000
☎ 61.3.6234.1219

Salamanca Wool Shop
69 Salamanca Place, Battery Pt
Hobart, TAS 7004
☎ 61.3.6234.1711

Tasmanian Wool Centre
48 Church Street
Ross, TAS 7209
☎ 61.3.6381.5466

Cranberry Crafts
71 Reibey Street
Ulverstone, TAS 7315
☎ 61.3.6425.1077

## Victoria

Sunspun Fine Yarns
185 Canterbury Road
Canterbury VIC 3126
☎ 61.3.9830.1609

A Little Patch of Country
63 Princes Hwy
Trafalgar, VIC 3824
☎ 61.3.5633.2311

AK Traditions
1209 Malvern Road
Melbourne, VIC 3144
☎ 61.3.9822.3393

Wool Baa
124 Bridport Street
Albert Park, Victoria 3206
Melbourne
☎ 61.3.9690.6633

**Western Australia**
Calico and Ivy
10 Glyde Street
☎ 61.8.9383.3794

Mosman Park
Perth, WA 6012
☎ 61.8.9383.3794

Bilby Yarns
Corner of Harrison Street and Hillary Street
Willagee, WA 6156
☎ 61.8.9331.8818

Margaret River Wool Company
2 Rosa Brook Road
Margaret River, WA 6285
☎ 61.8.9757.9493

# New Zealand

**(The country code for New Zealand is 64)**
Yarn=yarn

## Southland
BJ's Colourways & Collectibles
21 Price Street
Invercargill
☎ 64.3.215.7667

Creative Yarns & Knits
1145 Pukuatua St
Rotorua 3020
☎ 64.7.347.3568

## Wellington
Holland Road Yarn Company
281 Jackson Street, Petone 5012
☎ 64.4.891.0760

## North Otago
Enhance
127 Thames Street
Oamaru 9400
☎ 64.3.434.2144

# Acknowledgements

There are so many wonderful people to thank and many for whom I obtained my information:

Thank you to Ellie Bockert Augsburger, of Creative Digital Studios. She has the patience of a saint, which is what one needs to put a book together with such details!

Amanda and Kevin, who allowed me to use "Missed Your Exit" font. She has the coolest blog, so check her out!

Google translate, which allowed me to find words in other languages and translate.

Photos:
- Telephone Clip Art: clipartbest.com
- Black and white pictures of women knitting follow these guidelines: This work is in the public domain in the United States because it was published (or registered with the U.S. Copyright Office) before January 1, 1923.
- Pixabay, for allowing me the use of images free for commercial use.
- www.printableworldmap.com for map images.

Allen, Pam. Knitting for Dummies. New York, NY: Wiley, 2002. 64-65. Print.

Craft Yarn Council for their charts/abbreviations
Yarnstandards.com for their yarn and gauge ranges

# More Information/Contact

I are so excited to be publishing my first book on yarns shops around the world!

Your input is always important to me. If you find a shop that you would like to have published in my next edition, please visit me at www.peacockpressbooks.com or email at peacockpressbooks@gmail.com and let me know. If you find that an address has changed or a shop has closed, I want to know that as well.

Prefer to take an app along with you during your travels? I am working on that and expect it to be ready in by the summer of 2016! Also new, my Kindle edition available on Amazon!

Thank you for your purchase and I encourage your input, so feel free to contact me.


Lisa Prakash, Author

# Notes

www.ingramcontent.com/pod-product-compliance
Lightning Source LLC
Chambersburg PA
CBHW061640040426
42446CB00010B/1509